CHARGING INDIA

Developing E-Mobility Ecosystem

CHARGING INDIA

Developing E-Mobility Ecosystem

DR PARAG DIWAN

PENTAGON PRESS LLP

Charging India: Developing E-Mobility Ecosystem

DR PARAG DIWAN

ISBN 978-81-944659-6-6

First Published in 2021

Published by
PENTAGON PRESS LLP
206, Peacock Lane, Shahpur Jat,
New Delhi-110049
Phones: 011-64706243, 26491568
Telefax: 011-26490600
email: rajan@pentagonpress.in
website: www.pentagonpress.in

Printed at Aegean Offset Printers, Greater Noida, U.P.

CONTENTS

PREFACE

India is amongst the top polluting countries in the world and is home to 21 of the world's 30 cities with the worst air pollution. In some cities, the air is reported to be in the hazardous bracket of the Air Quality Index with reports suggesting that air pollution is the third biggest cause of death in the country.

India's transport demand has grown almost eight times since 1980 – more than any other Asian economy. Motorization rate, which is ownership of passenger car per 1000 inhabitants, is touching double digits in India. It follows a trend that being experienced by most developing economies. With approximately 200 million two-wheelers on road, India is by far the largest market, globally, for motorcycles and scooters and the numbers are on the rise. With the ownership of private vehicles increasing, the share of public transport has declined – from 69% in 1994 to 38% in 2007, especially in cities having more than four million population, leading to increased pollution.

With increasing freight movement in Indian urban cities, there is a need for a decarbonization of city systems to accommodate the growth in a sustainable manner. It is estimated that a significant cost in the delivery chain is in the last mile delivery. This is due to unpredictability of the delivery being successfully made due to the availability of the recipient, leading to multiple trips and circuitous non-efficient routing. It is estimated that freight vehicles contributing to about to 40% of air pollution in Indian cities and an unaccounted contribution to congestion levels. Adoption of new technology which is deployment of EV fleets for last mile delivery, the pollution levels can be decreased.

Given this backdrop, this book attempts to address the very fast-moving landscape of electric vehicles and electric vehicle charging in the country. With government creating frameworks like FAME-II which are helping the spread of electric vehicle revolution in the country. Over the past 5 years, the Indian electric mobility start-up landscape has grown significantly, with around 400+ electric mobility companies in the market currently.

This year, i.e., 2020 is predicted to be the tipping point for electric mobility. Though, India did have an electric vehicle called Reva in 2001, and it has taken 18 years for global companies to explore India as a potential market in the electric space, in the passenger and logistics transport vertical.

As our industry giants embark on a new paradigm – shape, structure, technology, material used in automobiles will also get revolutionised. The FAME India Scheme is serving as helping hand to all vehicle segments aims to put electric vehicles in the fast lane. Indian government to encourage faster adoption of electric and hybrid vehicles by way of offering upfront incentive on purchase of electric vehicles and by way of establishing necessary charging infrastructure for EV signalling a turning point in its clean energy policy.

The insights from this book explores the recent technology advancements, the low carbon footprint mobility segment, emerging EV Battery technologies, operating principles of Electric Motors, the changes in electric drivetrain systems, the regenerative braking system, Electric Vehicle Supply Equipment with various types of EV chargers and the establishment of an appropriate charging infrastructure.

The book further dwells into the major challenges and promulgation of appropriate EV policy sooner than later to keep the e-mobilisation on track. The industry players and manufacturers have unequivocally aligned with the government's vision. The mobility service providers must take various actions to ramp up industry by integrating by EVs.

While India going electric has created a momentum globally, setting up of achievable targets and goals should be the need of the hour and diligently working upon is another. With India's goal to reduce oil dependency and simultaneously solving the challenge of energy scarcity the move towards renewable and clean sources of energy are at the top of the national agenda and the road to electric mobility is one of the paths less travelled.

April 2020, Gurgaon **Dr Parag Diwan**

ACKNOWLEDGEMENT

This book has developed out of a series of blogs based on the research conducted on electric vehicle in India over past two years. I am thankful to several of young interns who helped me in conducting the research and putting together the data.

I acknowledge particularly the contribution of Somsuklo Biswas, Ayush Goel and Ankit Sinha who have assisted me in the initial research and developing the first drafts. The next generation of interns Deepak Sakthivel and Mohit Singhal helped me putting a more coherent form of draft and I duly acknowledge their contribution.

Further, I want to appreciate effort of Dr. Shyam Pandey who helped me a lot in developing the chapter on electric motors and drive trains. My research associate Arpita De did a lot of work in developing and creating infographics for the books.

Finally, I thank Suraj Anandan, my long-term colleague,not only for his crucial assistance in the initial research, preparation of the manuscript and his critical remarks on early draft but also for the secretarial assistance throughout this book project.

Dr Parag Diwan

CHAPTER ONE

INDIA'S QUEST FOR 100% ELECTRIC MOBILITY

Introduction

A century has gone by since the invention of internal combustion engine (ICE). However, the cars powered by them have over dependence on hydro-carbon fuels being therefore a major contributor to GHG emissions—accounting for nearly one fourth of total global energy related CO_2 emissions.

EV Charging Station

Given this context, electrification of transport in India can play a substantial role in mitigating emission and achieving the de-carbonization of the energy system. Therefore, today the auto industry finds itself at a crossroad due to recent advancements in

Electric Vehicle technology. This has created a new segment of low carbon footprint mobility. A move to electric vehicle (EVs) regime will be the key in urban areas for short-distance private vehicles as well as public transportation and freight delivery vehicles.

EVs are expected to give better efficiency. It is 95% more efficient than an ICE automobile. EV has only 20 moving parts as against 2000 which go into a traditional automobile, thus substantially reducing the energy conversion losses.

The Electrical Vehicle Initiatives (EVI), a multi-government policy forum dedicated to accelerate the deployment of EVs worldwide, has set a collective aspiring goal for their member countries of a 30% EV market share by 2030. World over, electric vehicles are backed by 30–40% subsidy, as the potential contribution of EVs to the de-carbonization of the global economy is substantial.

FAME India Scheme

(Faster Adoption and Manufacturing of Hybrid and Electric vehicles in India)

Government of India has notified FAME India Scheme for implementation with effect from 1st April 2015, with the objective to support hybrid/electric vehicles market development and Manufacturing eco-system. The scheme has 4 focus areas i.e. Technology development, Demand Creation, Pilot Projects and Charging Infrastructure.

The FAME India Scheme is aimed at incentivizing all vehicle segments i.e. 2 Wheeler, 3 Wheeler Auto, Passenger 4 Wheeler Vehicle, Light Commercial Vehicles and Buses. The scheme covers Hybrid & Electric technologies like Mild Hybrid, Strong Hybrid, Plug in Hybrid & Battery Electric Vehicles.

Electric Vehicles in the Indian Context

In line with the worldwide initiative for adoption of EVs, India too joined the bandwagon. Recently, it unveiled its grandiose plan of having 100% electric mobility by 2030. Through the framework,

Government of India wanted automakers to move to 100% manufacturing of EVs, in the next decade and half. However, in a typical flip flop, the government now is backtracking on the 2030 target and there is a confusion about whether an EV policy would be formulated or not.

Charging Station in India

Currently, there are only very a few manufacturers of EVs in India, the prominent being the Mahindra and Mahindra (M&M) and with their acquisition of REVA has marched ahead in this technology. They stand to benefit in the long term, as the government has clearly started the mandate and regulations for automakers to follow and switch to an alternate mobility based EV technology. However, in the recent government tender for both electric cars and buses under FAME scheme, TATA Motors has emerged as leading contender, outbidding the other Indian manufacturer. Also, there is an endeavor by India to get Tesla to establish a plant in India for higher end EVs.

Global Renaissance of Electric Vehicles

Historically EVs have been around, although they could not get into mainstream due to practical issues of range, speed and cost-effectiveness. The third generation of EVs today is marked by significant upgrade in battery capacity and technology and of course, substantial reduction in cost of ownership.

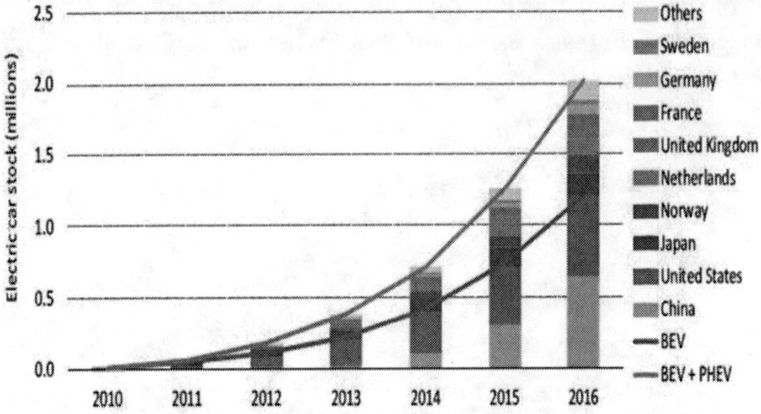

Notes: The electric car stock shown here is primarily estimated on the basis of cumulative sales since 2005. When available, stock numbers from official national statistics have been used, provided good consistency with sales evolutions.

Figure 1: Source: International Energy Agency Report, 2017, Global EV Outlook 2017

In 2016, over 750,000 sales marked record-high new electric car registrations worldwide. The transition to electric road transport technologies is gaining momentum across the world, due to its perceived reduction in carbon foot print. The global stock of electric cars has exceeded two million as the popularity increases in many countries. Norway achieved the highest electric car market share globally (29%) in 2016. In fact, China paved way for an extremely rapid market growth, from 100 thousand units in circulation in 2014 to 650 thousand units two years later. The provision of private and publicly accessible charging infrastructure has immensely helped this momentum. Last year, the number of publicly accessible charging points last reached 320,000 units globally, representing a 72% growth since 2015. These successes are driven by the multiple benefits EVs can bring to countries and its citizens: energy security, better urban air quality, reduction in noise pollution and greenhouse gas mitigation.

Rapid Growth in Global EV stock

In the next 10 to 20 years, the electric vehicle market is likely to get transition from early adopters to mass market adoption. From the indicators by OEM and announcement of country targets it seems to confirm these positive signals; signifying that cumulative electric car stock may range between 9 million and 20 million by 2020 and between 40 million and 70 million by 2025.

As the number of EVs increases, charging facilities and electricity consumption may impact the grid capacities and associated issues of the adequacy and quality of the power supply. EV propagation needs to be thought in a way that manages these issues. One way is to promote synergies with variable renewable energy sources. EVs could allow a greater integration of these energy sources in the power generation mix.

Can India Leapfrog to Electric Mobility?

Fast evolving technologies and engaging new business models for delivering new ways of mobility can potentially transform the world transportation scenario in years to come. The new mobility world order will be driven by quest to have:

- Clean yet cost-effective mobility services
- Creation of new jobs
- Reduction on oil dependence
- More efficient land use in cities
- Improvement in public health

In this backdrop, India is uniquely positioned to leapfrog into EV era of mobility due to a set of advantageous conditions and capabilities, be it IT and manufacturing, or PPP sector leadership, or even dynamic entrepreneurial culture wherein startups and new ventures in the mobility spaces are multiplying rapidly.

The confluence of low-cost technologies, smart design and integration, innovative business models, and supportive policies has established certain market segments to be economically viable today. Capturing those segments immediately can to a supportive foundation for the leap to happen.

As illustrated in Figure 2, the right integration and pursuance of opportunities among the core areas present India a better chance to achieve mobility leapfrog. These groups include system integration, shared infrastructure development and scaled manufacturing.

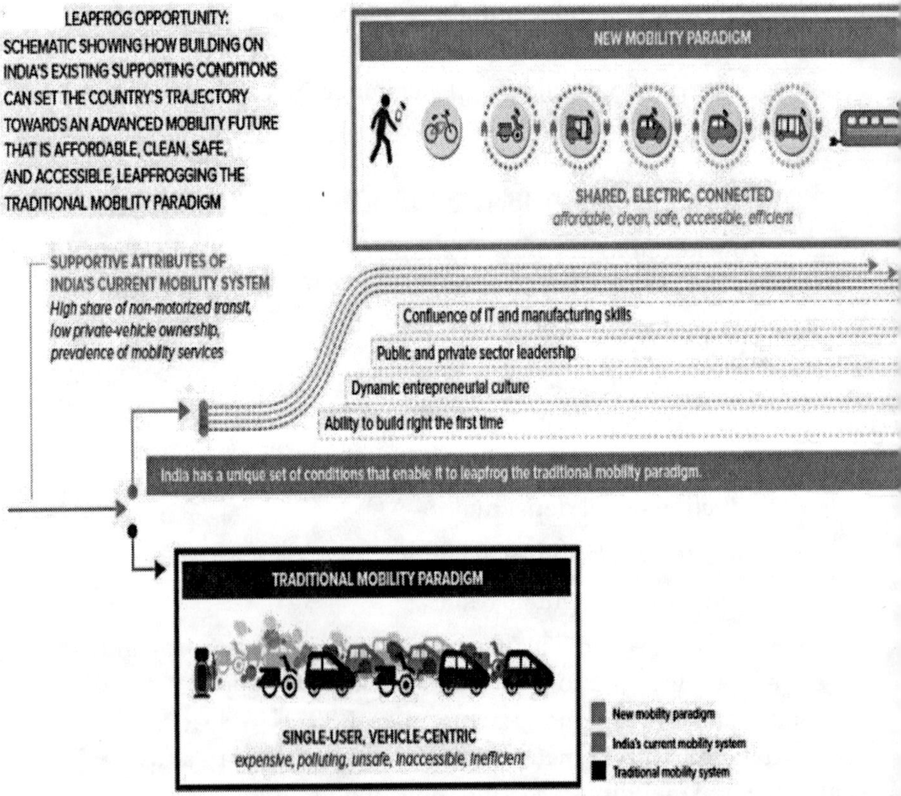

Figure 2: Source - India Leaps Ahead: Transformative Mobility Solutions for All, NITI Ayog Report May 2017

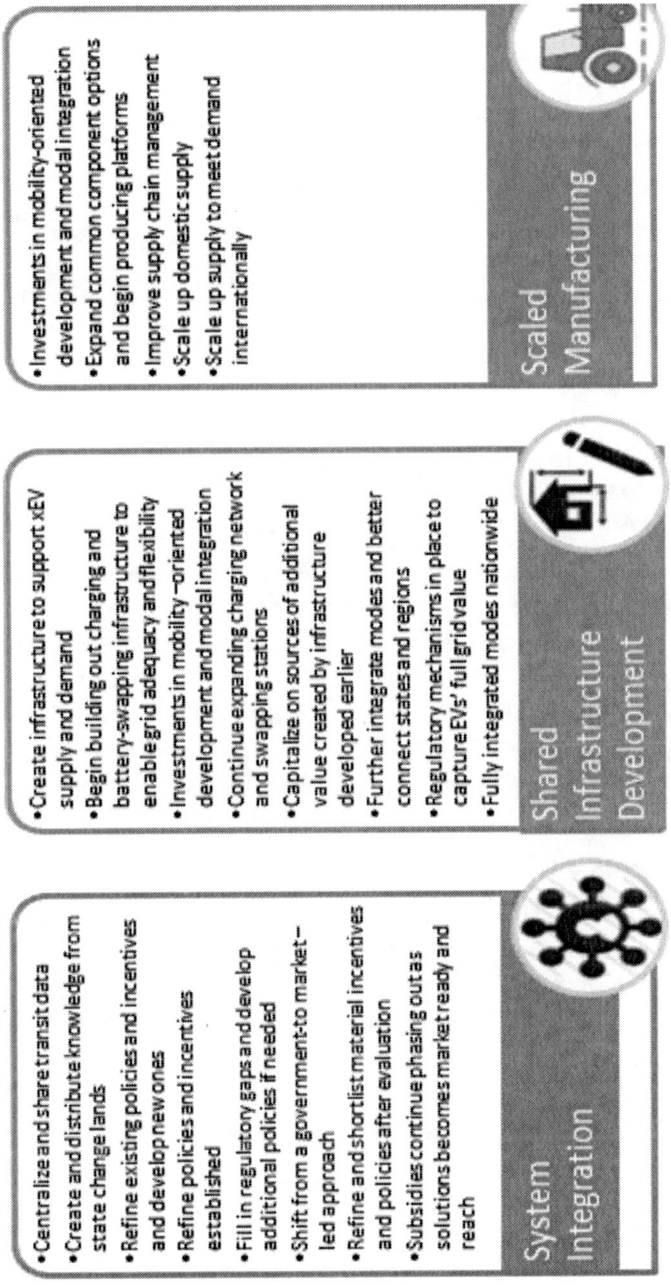
System Integration
• Centralize and share transit data
• Create and distribute knowledge from state change lands
• Refine existing policies and incentives and develop new ones
• Refine policies and incentives established
• Fill in regulatory gaps and develop additional policies if needed
• Shift from a government-to market – led approach
• Refine and shortlist material incentives and policies after evaluation
• Subsidies continue phasing out as solutions becomes market ready and reach
Shared Infrastructure Development
• Create infrastructure to support xEV supply and demand
• Begin building out charging and battery-swapping infrastructure to enable grid adequacy and flexibility
• Investments in mobility –oriented development and modal integration
• Continue expanding charging network and swapping stations
• Capitalize on sources of additional value created by infrastructure developed earlier
• Further integrate modes and better connect states and regions
• Regulatory mechanisms in place to capture EVs' full grid value
• Fully integrated modes nationwide
Scaled Manufacturing
• Investments in mobility-oriented development and modal integration
• Expand common component options and begin producing platforms
• Improve supply chain management
• Scale up domestic supply
• Scale up supply to meet demand internationally

Figure 3

Challenges in Achieving Full Electric Mobility by 2030

Battery Cost

One of the biggest challenges for adoption of electric vehicles in India is its price. Therefore, the TCO (Total Cost of Ownership) of electric vehicles has to be comparable or only slightly higher than an IC powered vehicle for the price and operative cost sensitive Indian owner. Therefore, one of the imperatives is to have the significant reduction in battery cost, which means it has to be made locally.

However, battery cost may no longer be an issue given the falling battery prices. The price has fallen from $1000 to $600 per battery in 2012 to $250 in 2017 and likely to go down to as low as $100 by 2024 per KWh. Therefore, in the next 5 years, capital costs of EVs will be less than that of petrol vehicles—with acceptable range and operational costs at a fraction of that ICE based vehicles. It is very important for India to start a massive battery manufacturing program or else we would simply swap the crude oil import bill by battery and associated sub-systems. In this context, the recent joint venture between Suzuki Motor Corp, Toshiba Corporation and Denso Corporation to set up a lithium-ion battery unit in India augers a bright way forward for others to follow suit.

Subsystems and Components

On the other hand, the Indian auto components industry would have undergo a metamorphosis to supply many of the components and subsystems for EVs. Auto-ancillaries need to adapt, upgrade and scale up for the EV future under *"Make in India"* program and seek preferential investments.

Charging Infrastructure and Grid Connectivity

One of the major hurdles in the adoption of EVs is likely to be the battery-charging infrastructure. Another possible show-stopper to dominance of EVs can be India's inability to generate enough

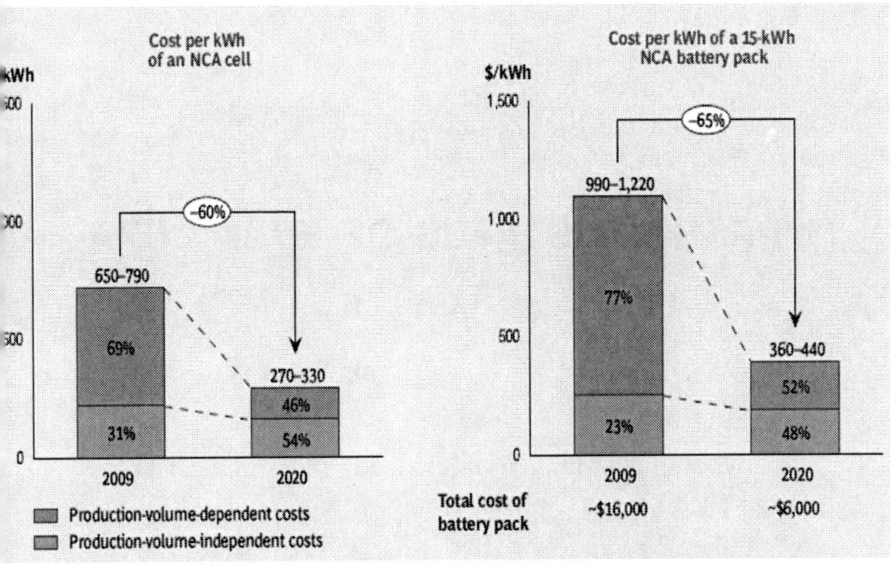

Figure 4: Production of 500 batteries in 2009 and 73 mn. cells and 1.1 mn. batteries in 2020. Source- Argonne National Laboratory; BCG analysis

electricity to propel its mobility. To encourage commuters to switch to electric cars without offering a subsidy and build a model that makes economic sense and at the same time enables it to scale early are vital in India's scenario. This will require battery charging infrastructure to be connected to power distribution system, perhaps using off-grid renewable energy sources.

Biggest need of nation, however, is to have charging stations across the length and breadth of the country to allow for easy adoption of electric vehicles. A pilot has commenced in Delhi NCR to have 4000 charging stations in near future.

To conclude, a convergence of government policy, cost reduction, local technology upgrade and charging infrastructure would be needed for India to leapfrog to Electric. If nothing else, it will help kick-start the transition in Indian automotive industry and spawn many new innovative startups.

CHAPTER TWO

PRESENT STATUS OF EV IN INDIA

Introduction

The Government of India has signaled the beginning of a new era of mobility for India. Global technology trends and India's rapidly growing economy have led to focus on electrification of transportation as the primary technology pathway to achieve this transformation. This intersection presents India with a powerful but perishable opportunity to emerge as a global leader in new mobility solutions and battery manufacturing, positioning India for durable economic growth and global competitiveness. India is uniquely positioned to deploy electric vehicles (EVs) at scale, leapfrogging traditional mobility models that perpetuate congestion, air pollution and oil import dependence while driving down the costs of batteries through economies of scale even faster than the rate at which current projections anticipate.

Government Initiatives

- In 2012, the National Electric Mobility Mission Plan (NEMMP) 2020 was established to promote hybrid and electric vehicles.
- Under the NEMMP 2020, an incentive scheme, Faster Adoption and Manufacturing of Hybrid and Electric Vehicles (FAME Phase 1&2), was launched in 2015 to reduce the upfront purchase price of hybrid and electric vehicles and to stimulate their early adoption.

- In early 2018, the Ministry of Power launched the new National Electric Mobility Programme to focus on creating the charging infrastructure and a policy framework to set a target of more than 30% electric vehicles by 2030.
- The Programme will be implemented by Energy Efficiency Services Limited (EESL) which will aggregate demand by procuring electric vehicles in bulk to get economies of scale.
- Ministry of Power (MoP) has notified the charging infrastructure for electric vehicles-guidelines and standards on 14th December 2018.
- Special incentives for Indigenous OEM and EV manufacturers were announced under FAME.
- Many state governments like Delhi, Maharashtra, Tamilnadu have announced state policies for adoption of EV.

Ministries and agencies involved in Electric Vehicle programme in India

At the central level, several ministries and departments have been involved in supporting the electric mobility transition, including the Ministry of Road Transport and Highways, Department of Heavy Industry, Department of Industrial Policy and Promotion, Ministry of Finance, Ministry of Housing and Urban Affairs, Ministry of Power, Ministry of New and Renewable Energy, Department of Science and Technology and NITI Aayog. Additionally, 27 states have formulated strategies for transforming their mobility systems and several states have formulated or are in the process of formulating their EV policies.

National Electric Mobility Mission Plan (NEMMP)

Government of India launched the National Electric Mobility Mission Plan (NEMMP) 2020 in 2013. It aims to achieve national fuel security by promoting hybrid and electric vehicles in the country. There is an ambitious target to achieve 6-7 million sales of hybrid and electric vehicles year on year from 2020 onwards. To support this initiative Government aims to provide fiscal and monetary incentives to kick start this nascent technology. With the support from the Government, the cumulative sale is expected to reach 15-16 Million by 2020. It is expected to save 9500 Million Liters of crude oil equivalent to Rs. 62000 Cr. savings. Government has launched the scheme namely Faster Adoption and Manufacturing of (Hybrid &) Electric Vehicles (FAME India) under NEMMP 2020 in the Union Budget for 2015-16 with an initial outlay of Rs. 795 Cr. It is envisaged that early market creation through demand incentive, in-house technology development and domestic production will help industry reach a self-sufficient economy of scale in the long run by around the year 2020

FAME 1 (Faster Adoption and Manufacturing of Electric Vehicles 1)

The release of the Faster Adoption and Manufacturing of Electric Vehicles (FAME) Scheme provides an opportunity to reflect on India's recent progress and the required next steps for moving towards an electric mobility future. Phase I of the FAME-India Scheme was launched on April 1st, 2015 and extended to March 31, 2019. Its original time period was two years but it was extended three times. The scheme was implemented with an outlay of Rs 795 crore. Approximately 2,18,625 Electric Vehicles were 'promoted' by FAME I till July 2018 and the main objective is to provide demand incentives. The mother programme of FAME—the National Electric Mobility Mission Plan (NEMMP) 2020 was launched in 2013 to achieve sales of six-seven million units of electric vehicles and thus to realize fossil fuel saving of 2.2 to 2.5 million tonnes.

Initial area coverage of FAME phase 1

1) Cities under "Smart Cities" initiatives
2) Major metro agglomerations – Delhi NCR, Greater Mumbai, Kolkata, Chennai, Bengaluru, Hyderabad, Ahmedabad

3) All State and other Urban Agglomerations/Cities with 1 million+ population (as per 2011 census
4) Cities of the North Eastern States

Fund Allocation of FAME 1

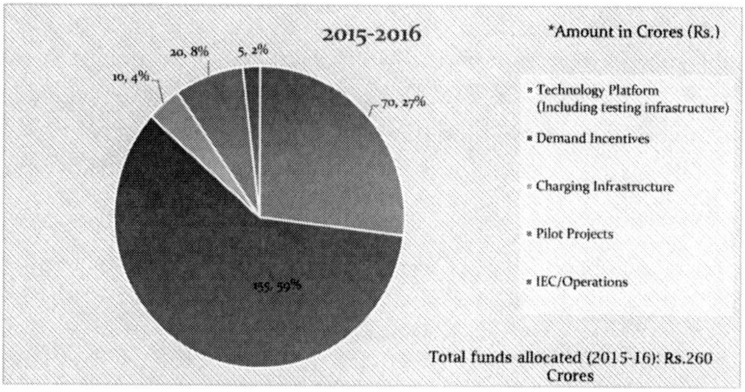

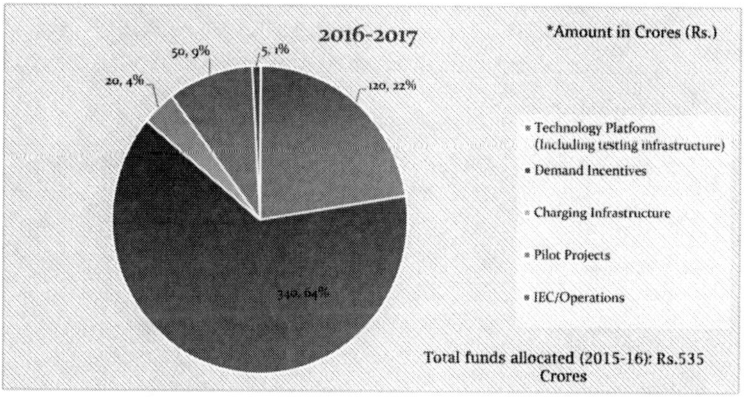

FAME 2 (Faster Adoption and Manufacturing of Electric Vehicles 2)

The second phase is an expanded version of the first phase. FAME India Phase II has a total outlay of Rs 10000 Crores over the period of three years from 1st April 2019 to 2022. Allocation for the scheme for 2019-20 is estimated to be at Rs 1,500-crore; Rs 5,000 crore in 2020-21 and Rs 3,500 crore in 2021-22. FAME-II will cover buses using EV technology; electric, plug-in hybrid and strong hybrid four wheelers; electric three-wheelers including e-rickshaws and electric two-wheelers. For the overall monitoring, sanctioning and implementation of the scheme, an inter-ministerial empowered committee – 'Project Implementation and Sanctioning Committee' (PISC) that is headed by the heavy industry secretary, has be constituted. In early 2018, the Ministry of Power launched the new National Electric Mobility Programme with broad objectives. Here, the focus is for establishing the electric charging infrastructure and a policy framework to set realize more than 30% electric vehicles by 2030.

The scheme is proposed to be implemented through the following verticals:

1) Demand Incentives
2) Establishment of network of Charging Stations
3) Administration of Scheme including Publicity, IEC (Information, Education & Communication) activities.

Fund Allocation for FAME 2:

Sl. No.	*Components*	*2019-20*	*2020-21*	*2021-22*	*Total Fund requirement in crores*
1	Demand Incentives	822	4587	3187	8596
2	Charging Infrastructure	300	400	300	1000
3	Administrative Expenditure including Publicity, ICE activities	12	13	13	38
	Total for FAME-II	1134	5000	3500	9634
4	Committed expenditure of Phase-I	366	0	0	366
	Total	1500	5000	3500	10000

Various Initiatives by Ministries and other Government institutions

Ministry of Power (MoP):

1. MoP issued a policy on charging infrastructure to enable faster adoption of EVs. The policy permits private charging at residences and offices where tariff for supply of electricity to EV charging station shall not be more than the average cost of supply plus 15 percent
2. MoP issued a clarification stating that charging EVs is considered a service, not a sale of electricity, meaning that no license is required to operate EV charging stations

Ministry of Road Transport and Highways (MoRTH):

1. MoRTH announced that battery-operated vehicles, both private and commercial, will be given green license plates (GSR 749 (E))
2. MoRTH announced that it will facilitate the import of 2,500 electric vehicles compliant with international standards without the need for homologation (GSR 870 (E))
3. MoRTH announced that all battery-operated, ethanol-powered and methanol-powered transport vehicles will be exempted from the requirement of permits (S.O. 5333(E))
4. MoRTH amended Central Motor Vehicles Rules (CMVR), 1989 to allow driving licenses to be given for age group 16–18 years to drive gearless electric scooters and bikes up to 4 kWh battery size (GSR 1225 (E))

Ministry of Housing and Urban Affairs (MoHUA):

1. MoHUA released an amendment of building code and town planning rules for provisioning of EV charging stations in private and commercial buildings

Ministry of Finance (MoF):

1. MoF rationalized the customs duty for all categories of vehicles, battery packs and cells to support Make in India

and incentivize uptake of electric vehicles (Notification no. 03/2019-Customs)

2. Reduced GST rates for the purchase of electric vehicles from 12% to 5% (Financial Budget 2019)
3. Announced an income tax rebate of Rs. 1,50,000 on purchase of electric vehicles (Financial Budget 2019)

NITI Aayog:

1. The Cabinet approved the National Mission on Transformative Mobility and Battery Storage, which will drive clean, connected, shared, sustainable and holistic mobility initiatives
2. The Mission aims at creation of a Phased Manufacturing Programme (PMP) for five years, to support setting up of large-scale, export-competitive integrated batteries and cell-manufacturing giga plants in India, as well as localizing production across the entire electric vehicle value chain
3. NITI Aayog released a concessionaire Agreement for public private partnership in operation and maintenance of electric buses in cities through Operating Expenditure (OPEX) model. This would reduce the requirement of upfront capital as the lease would be signed on a per-kilometer basis

Department of Heavy Industry (DHI):

1. The Cabinet approved FAME II, the second phase of the scheme for Faster Adoption and Manufacturing of (Hybrid &) Electric Vehicles in India
2. The scheme has a total outlay of Rs. 10,000 crores, to be used for upfront incentives on the purchase of EVs as well as supporting the development of charging infrastructure

Department of Science and Technology (DST):

1. DST launched a Grand Challenge for developing the Indian Standards for Electric Vehicle Charging Infrastructure
2. Additionally, Bureau of Indian Standards (BIS) has notified

general requirements for EV charging based on CCS & CHAdeMO charging standards

Indian Space Research Organisation (ISRO):

1. Indian Space Research Organisation (ISRO) issued a request for quotation (RFQ) document for commercialization of indigenously developed lithium-ion battery technology. Thus far, ten firms have been shortlisted for the transfer of technology.

Various state policies regarding EV

States	*Key policy elements/Targets*
Andhra Pradesh Electric Mobility Policy 2018–2023	• Goal of 10 lakh EVs by 2024 • Goal of 1 lakh slow and fast EV charging stations by 2024 • Government plans to stop registration of petrol and diesel cars by 2024 in the upcoming capital city of Amaravati • All government vehicles, including corporations, boards and government ambulances to be electric by 2024
NCT of Delhi Draft Electric Vehicle Policy 2018	• Aims at 25% of new vehicle registrations to be electric by 2023 • 50% of entire public transport targeted to be electric by 2023 • Proposes a feebate to fund a high proportion of the incentives • Encourages the reuse and recycling of EV batteries that have reached the end of their lives
Karnataka Electric Vehicles Manufacturing Policy 2018	• 100% of three and four-wheelers moving goods will be encouraged to transition to electric by 2030 • Incentives for first 100 fast chargers • Encourages startups to develop business models focused on supporting economic applications for EVs
Kerala Electric Vehicle Policy 2018	• Target of bringing 1 million EVs to the state by 2022 • By 2022, the state aims to pilot a fleet of 200,000 two-wheelers, 50,000 three-wheelers,

States	*Key policy elements/Targets*
	1,000 goods carriers, 3,000 buses and 100 ferry boats
Maharashtra Electric Vehicle & Related Infrastructure Policy 2018	• Target to increase number of EV registrations in Maharashtra to 5 lakhs • Generate an investment of Rs. 25,000 crores for the manufacturing of EVs • Create jobs for 1 lakh people
Telangana Electric Vehicle Policy Draft 2017	• Telangana State Transport Corporation to set a target of 100% electric buses by 2030 for intracity, intercity and interstate transport • Telangana Government will set up first 100 fast charging stations in GHMC and other cities in a phased manner
Uttar Pradesh Electric Vehicles Manufacturing Policy 2018	• Goal of 1,000 electric buses deployed in the state by 2030 • Target of achieving 100% electrification of autorickshaws, cabs, school buses/vans, etc., by 2030 in five cities: GB Nagar, Lucknow, Kanpur, Varanasi and Ghaziabad
Uttarakhand EV Manufacturing, EV Usage Promotion & Related Services Infrastructure Policy 2018	• Aimed at making Uttarakhand a preferred destination for investment in EV manufacturing capacity • Special focus on developing green highways in Dehradun, Haridwar, Rishikesh, Haldwani, Rudrapur and Kashipur • Term loans in the range of Rs.100 million to Rs.500 million will be provided to micro, small and medium enterprises interested in manufacturing EVs

Industry Initiatives

Vehicle Manufacturing and Sales

According to market estimates, in financial year 2018 electric two-wheeler sales almost doubled to 54,800 compared to the previous financial year. Electric two-wheelers have been leading the EV market; estimates suggest they account for 98% of the country's EV sales. Manufacturers, established and new, continue to/are starting to invest in the Indian EV market through fund infusion, investments in start-ups and expansion plans. Companies are designing and testing products suitable for the Indian market with a key focus on electric two-wheelers and three-wheelers. OEMs have been forging partnerships with state and city governments such as Delhi, Pune, Ahmedabad and Bengaluru to augment the public transport system to bolster shared mobility. As recently as March 2019, over 100 companies showcased electric vehicles of all types at the India E-Vehicle Show.

Components and Battery Manufacturing

The Indian government reduced tariffs on imported parts of EVs in January 2019 to boost assembly in India. The automobile industry has indicated that this will trigger investments in critical components. Battery manufacturers have announced major joint venture investments to produce both battery cells and packs in India with an aim to contribute to the 'Make in India' drive. Several manufacturers, energy solution providers and start-ups have announced their plans to make lithium-ion batteries in India through R&D centers and lithium-ion battery manufacturing plants. India is likely to see a surge in new cell manufacturing units in India with key players lining up their long-term plans. Ten companies have come forward to adopt Indian Space Research Organisation's (ISRO) cell chemistry for commercial applications.

Charging Infrastructure and Battery Swapping

Significant investment is being mobilized by the private sector to manufacture and install electric vehicle supply equipment (EVSE) infrastructure across India. This includes charging and battery swapping technologies. Both charging and swapping solutions are supported by business model innovation that enables high utilization of infrastructure. Plans are underway to fuel EVs with clean power, with industry players exploring solar-plus-EV technology in Mumbai and beyond. Moreover, the Indian Railways has announced its intention to allocate space for electric vehicle charging stations at their station parking lots. Railways authorities aim to invite private sector participation by issuing tenders to create this infrastructure. Public sector units in India have signed several

Memorandums of Understanding (MoUs) with aggregators to develop dedicated EV charging stations across Indian cities.

Mobility Services

Mobility service providers around the world and in India are testing EV solutions in anticipation of wider-scale deployment. Compelling economics are encouraging aggregators and drivers to act on EVs' low operating costs, which can offset their capital cost premium. Despite competitive economics, persistent challenges exist including the operational mandates of service vehicles, risk aversion from drivers and fleet operators, and the first cost difference between ICEs and EVs. In order to address some of these challenges and capture the economic advantages of EVs, taxi aggregators and car rental platforms have formed partnerships with original equipment manufacturers (OEMs) to manufacture and test fit to purpose vehicles.

CHAPTER THREE

BATTERY IS THE HEART OF ELECTRIC VEHICLE

Introduction

No doubt, the heart of an EV is its battery. Unlike the batteries in traditional cars, which primarily serve to start the engine and run accessories like the lights, wipers, radio and/or ACs, the battery in an EV runs everything.

Importantly, it runs the electric motor, so it needs to be powerful and long-lasting enough to take drivers where they need to go with a minimum of recharging. Until recently, no reliable, mass-producible batteries were manufactured that could make electric cars competitive with IC cars.

About two decades ago, the interest in EVs got renewed, and the development of higher energy density batteries came to the research forefront. Recently, the battery technology has made mass-production electric cars a reality, thanks to the technology advancement. It is an evolving technology driven to new heights by companies like Tesla, Nissan et al. As a result, today EVs have not only become feasible, but they are now rolling off the assembly lines of major automobile manufacturers.

Historical Overview

Ever since the discovery of electricity, humans have sought to have simple yet portable source of current in form of a battery. Though, the challenge was that it had to balance; power, weight, cost, and some other factors. Scientists have worked for over a century to get to today's level of battery efficiency which included many trade-offs. Highlighted below are some of the important milestones of this journey.

Major Milestones in Battery Development

- **Voltaic Pile (1799):** Italian physicist Alessandro Volta invented the first battery, known as the voltaic pile. It consisted of pairs of copper and zinc discs piled on top of each other, separated by a layer of cloth or cardboard soaked in brine (i.e., the electrolyte).
- **Daniell Cell (1836):** About 40 years later, a British Chemist John F Daniell created a new cell using a copper pot filled with copper sulfate solution, which was further immersed in an earthenware container filled with sulfuric acid and a zinc electrode.
- **Lead-acid (1859):** French Physicist Gaston Plante invented the first rechargeable battery based on lead-acid, which is low cost and it can supply high surge currents
- **Nickel Cadmium (1899):** NiCad battery was invented by Waldemar Jungner, a Sweden Scientist. Though. NiCad helped to pave the way for modern technology, it got outmoded due to cadmium's toxicity.
- **Alkaline (1950s):** The modern alkaline battery was invented by Canadian Engineer. Lewis Urry. Even today, alkaline batteries have been widely used in regular household items.
- **Nickel-Metal Hydride (1989):** NiMH battery formulation uses a hydrogen-absorbing alloy leading to more environmental friendly and helps to increase the energy density. NiMH batteries are used in power tools, digital cameras, and some other electronic devices.
- **Lithium Ion (1991):** In li-ion batteries, graphite is a common material for use in the anode and the electrolyte is most often a

type of lithium salt suspended in an organic solvent. SONY commercialized this technology. It has high energy density and has a number of specific cathode formulations for different applications.

Evolution of Batteries over the years for EV application

Several battery chemistries have been introduced including improved lead–acid, nickel–cadmium, nickel–zinc, NiMH, zinc–air, sodium–sulfur, sodium–metal chloride, Li-ion batteries in the EV segments.

The experimentation with battery chemistries is due to fact that, for EVs there are several factors that could affect battery choice, including cost. However, two factors that determine the fit and use of rechargeable batteries specifically are:

1. **Specific Energy**—*the amount of energy a battery holds in total.*
2. **Specific Power**—*the amount of current a battery can supply for a given use.*

It is depicted in the info-graphic Figure 5:

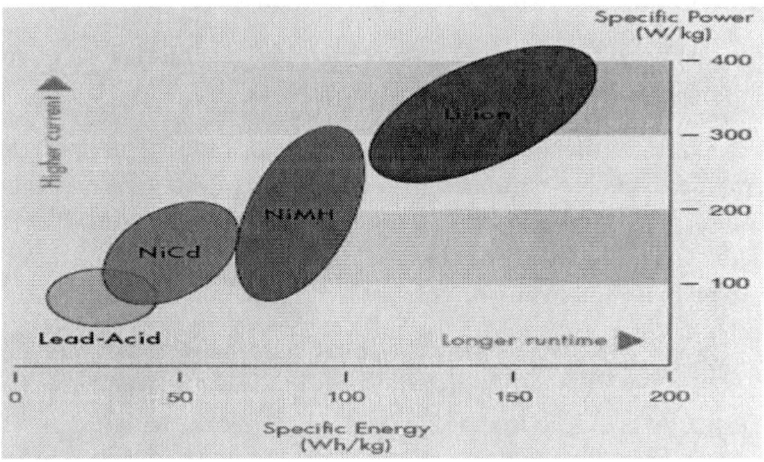

Figure 5: Source: visualcapitalist.com

Reviewed below are some of the battery technologies being

used in the EVs and the state-of-art, emerging technological development in the field.

Lead-acid

There are 2 types of lead-acid batteries, automobile engine starter batteries, and deep cycle batteries. Automobile alternators are designed to provide starter batteries high charge rates for fast charges, while deep cycle batteries used for electric vehicles like golf carts or e-rickshaws. Historically, most EVs have used lead-acid batteries due to their mature technology, high availability, and low cost.

Lead-acid batteries in EV applications end up being a significant (25–50%) portion of the final vehicle mass. Like all batteries, they have significantly lower energy density than fossil fuels—in this case, 30–40 Wh/kg. However, due to lighter drive-train in EV, higher weight of batteries is partly compensated. Still, with the best batteries EVs of a range comparable to IC vehicles tend to lead to higher weight. Recent advances in battery efficiency, capacity, materials, safety, toxicity and durability are likely to allow these superior characteristics to be applied in car-sized EVs.

Lead-acid batteries powered such early-modern EVs as the original versions of the EV1 and the RAV4 EV.

Due to further developments in EV application, VRLA batteries emerged. A valve-regulated lead-acid battery (VRLA battery) also called sealed lead-acid (SLA) battery. Another type of VRLA battery is the Gel and Absorbent Glass Mat (AGM) types of VRLA which can be mounted in any orientation with minimal maintenance.

In India, most EVs are either three wheeled rickshaws or two wheeler. Both the segments are highly price sensitive. The fact of the matter is that, in India, lead-acid takes the cake with its definite pricing edge. The initial cost of a lead-acid battery pack is much cheaper than its equitable lithium-ion battery (LIB) pack.

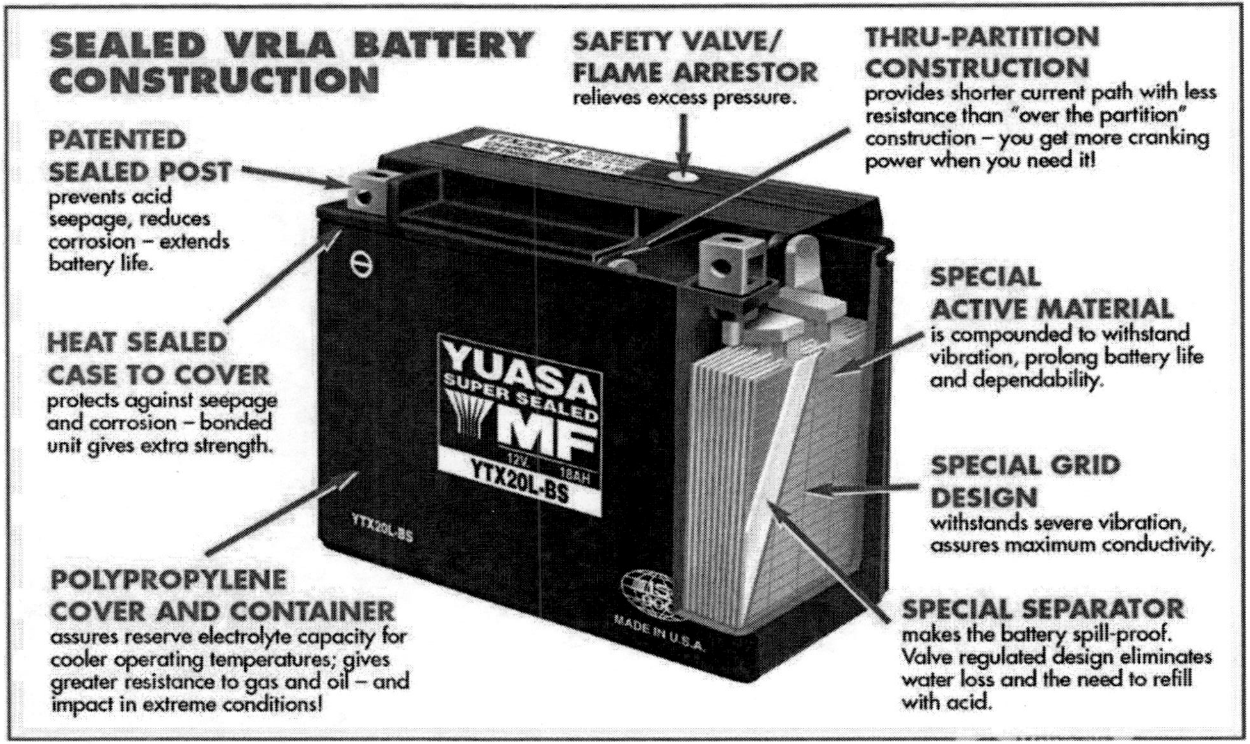

Figure 6: VRLA Battery Construction, Source: Google

Although, the advantages of LIB may justify its price on many levels, the Indian consumer is wary of having to shell out this additional investment in the aforesaid segments.

Specially developed VRLA batteries for EVs application are widely available and are considered as a competitively priced product, the cost of initial purchase is affordable to an EV owner and in the long run, replacements are also favorable in terms of their price. Also, the lack of lithium-in India and the fact that lithium-ion technology for electric cars is a whole new territory and can't be integrated into current manufacturing regimes.

NiCad battery

The nickel–cadmium batteries (NiCad) is a type of rechargeable battery using nickel oxide hydroxide and metallic cadmium as electrodes and were about 50% more energy dense than the lead-acid. NiCad batteries can be made in a wide range of sizes and capacities. Compared with other types of rechargeable cells, they offer good cycle life and performance at low temperatures with a fair capacity but their significant advantage is the ability to deliver practically their full rated capacity at high discharge rates (discharging in one hour or less). However, the materials are more costly than that of the lead–acid battery, and the cells have high self-discharge rates.

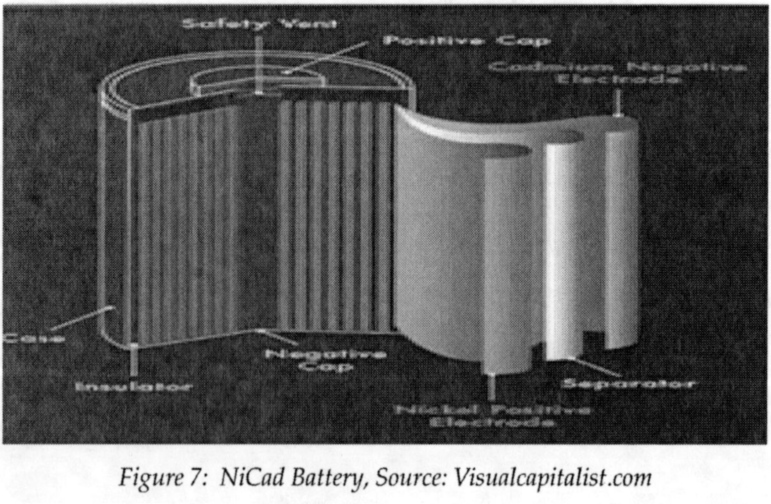

Figure 7: NiCad Battery, Source: Visualcapitalist.com

NiCad was state of the art batteries all through the 1990's. They were used in quite a few EVs in France and US. However, the environmental impact of the disposal of the toxic metal cadmium has contributed to waning of this technology for EV applications.

Nickel Metal Hydride

The demise of NiCad batteries for EVs led to development of Nickel-Metal-Hydride (NiMH) batteries which are about 200% as energy-dense as lead-acid. These were first used by Toyota Prius and Honda Insight hybrid electric cars. However, an NiMH electric car battery pack would simply be too heavy to achieve range improvements.

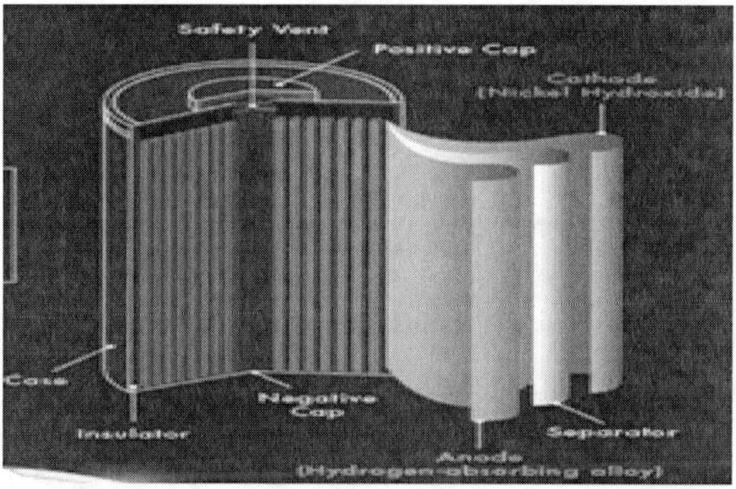

Figure 8: Construction of NiMH batteries, Source: visualcapitalist.com

NiMH batteries are now considered a relatively mature technology. While less efficient (60–70%) in charging and discharging than lead-acid, they have an energy density of 40–80 Wh/kg, far higher than lead-acid. When used properly, NiMH batteries can have exceptionally long lives, as has been demonstrated in their use in hybrid cars and surviving NiMH RAV4 EVs that still operate well after 100,000 miles (160,000 km) and over a decade of service.

NiMH battery used in the second generation EV-1 and worked very well. By 2008, more than two million hybrid cars worldwide were manufactured with NiMH batteries.

However, the status of NiMH batteries in EV segment diminished over time due to the increased popularity of lithium-ion batteries.

Li-ion battery

A lithium-ion battery (Li-ion/LIB) is a type of rechargeable battery in which lithium- ions move from the negative electrode to the positive electrode during discharge and back when charging. Li-ion batteries use an intercalated lithium compound as one electrode material, compared to the metallic lithium used in a non-rechargeable lithium battery. The electrolyte, which allows for ionic movement, and the two electrodes are the constituent components of a Li-ion cell.

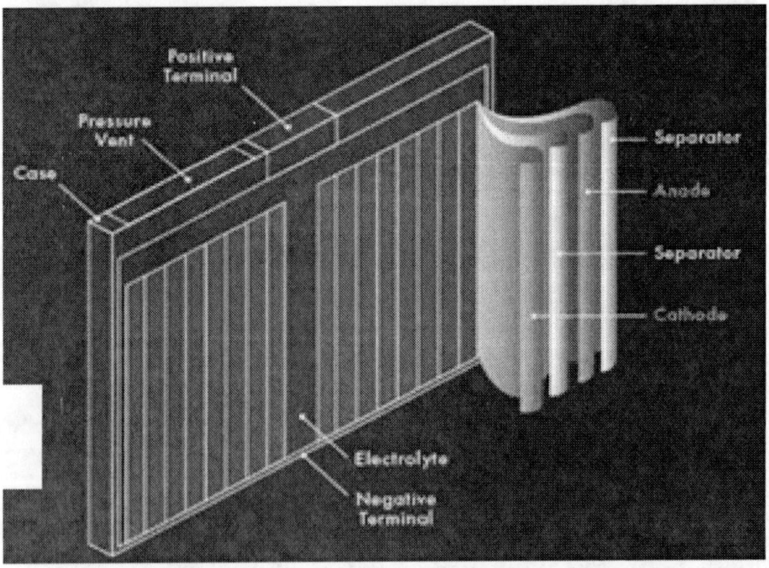

Figure 9: A lithium-ion battery (Li-ion/LIB), Source: visualcapitalist.com

Lithium batteries were initially developed in the 1970s by using titanium (IV) sulfide and lithium metal as the electrodes. However, titanium disulfide was a poor choice, since it has to be synthesized under completely sealed conditions, also being quite expensive. When exposed to air, titanium disulfide reacts to form hydrogen sulfide compounds which are toxic to most animals.

Batteries with metallic lithium electrodes presented safety issues, as lithium is a highly reactive element; it burns in normal atmospheric conditions because of spontaneous reactions with water and oxygen. As a result, research moved to develop batteries in which, instead of metallic lithium, only lithium compounds are present, being capable of accepting and releasing lithium ions. Currently used Lithium compounds in LIB is shown in Figure 10.

At first LIB were not cheap. Actually, the initial commercial LIBs in the mid-90s costed upwards of $3,000 per kWh of energy. However, with technology and manufacturing innovations, the cost of LIBs has come down dramatically, making it the battery of choice for EV applications.

By developing mass scale LIB production in its Giga-factory, Tesla now claims that a Tesla Model S battery cost is $240 per kWh and that the expected cost for a Model 3 is $190 per kWh. At $240 kWh, lithium-ions become competitive with $3/gallon gas. At $150, they are even competitive with $2 gas.

Therefore, it is expected that for next 5–10 years, the LIBs will rule the roost in so far their application in EV segment is concerned. In fact, experts estimate that lithium-ions will continue to increase capacity by 6–7% annually for a number of years.

This would only be possible with constant improvement of LIBs based on multiple advances. Some of these are as follows:

Efficient Manufacturing

Tesla has already demonstrated significant advances in battery design and production through its Giga-factory. Some of the other players are going to follow the game by better engineering and manufacturing processes, wider and longer cell design allows more

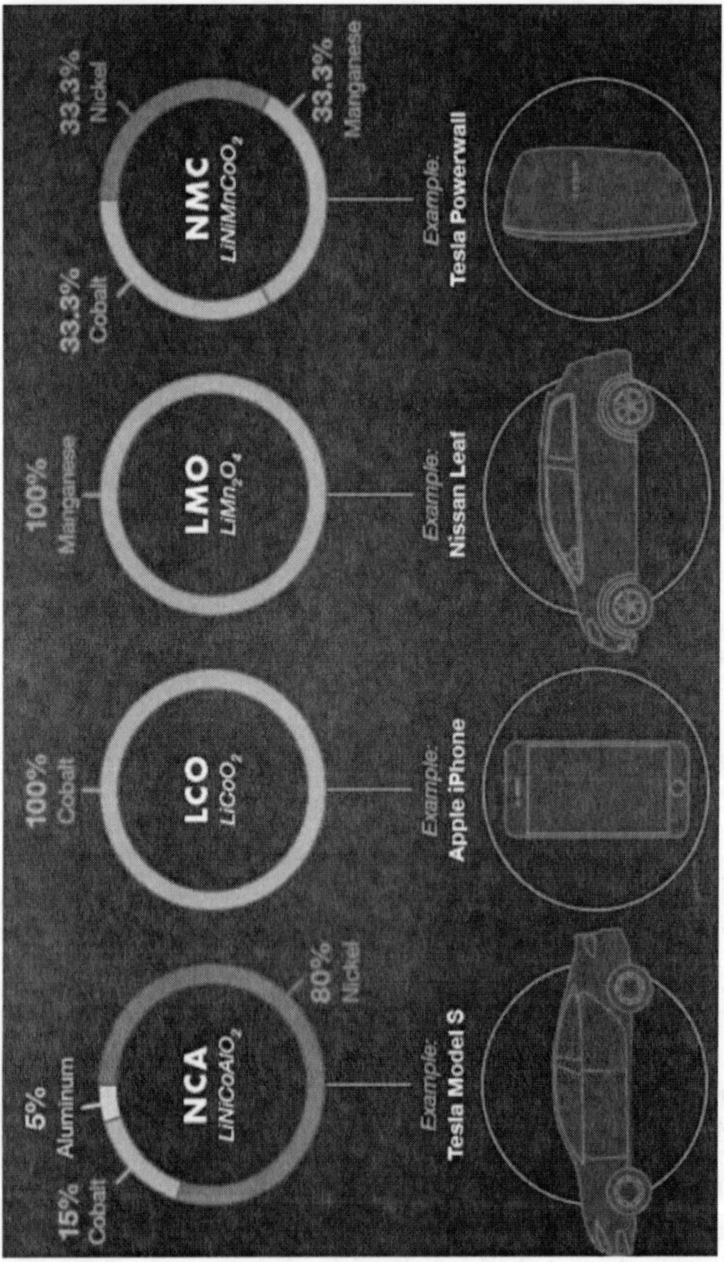

Figure 10: Lithium compounds in LIB batteries, Source: visualcapitalist.com

materials packaged into each cell and new battery cooling system allows to fit more cells into battery pack.

Better Cathodes: Cathode optimization by manipulating the relative quantities of cobalt, aluminum, manganese and nickel into LIBs, it has significantly increased the energy density. Research is going on to find the materials that store maximum amount of ions.

Better Anodes: Using silicon anodes instead of current graphite ones can increase battery capacity by ten folds. But, silicon anodes have a problem of bloating in size, thus damaging the anode and finishing battery life. Some new approaches to make silicon anode workable include:

- Encasing silicon in a graphene "cage" to prevent cracking after expansion.
- Using silicon nano-wires, which can better handle the volume change.
- Adding silicon in tiny amounts in current graphite anodes.

Solid-State Lithium-Ion: High performance batteries can be solid state ionic devices. To achieve the higher energy density in lower cost, development of a solid state electrolyte is essential. In 2017, a

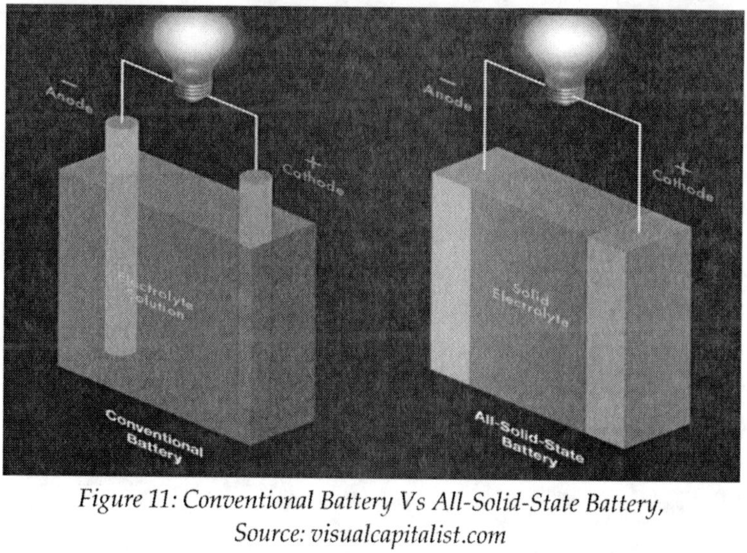

Figure 11: Conventional Battery Vs All-Solid-State Battery, Source: visualcapitalist.com

new solid-state battery has been unveiled, using glass electrolytes and an alkali-metal anode consisting of lithium, sodium. This design could increase energy density, but it still has some problems to resolve, such as ions moving too slowly through the solid electrolyte.

Emerging EV Battery Technologies

Currently, there are several approaches to battery innovations that may lead to making EVs ubiquitous. Certainly, path to commercialization is long, hard and may have pitfalls too. The graphic below summarizes the possible paradigm shift in the EV battery approach.

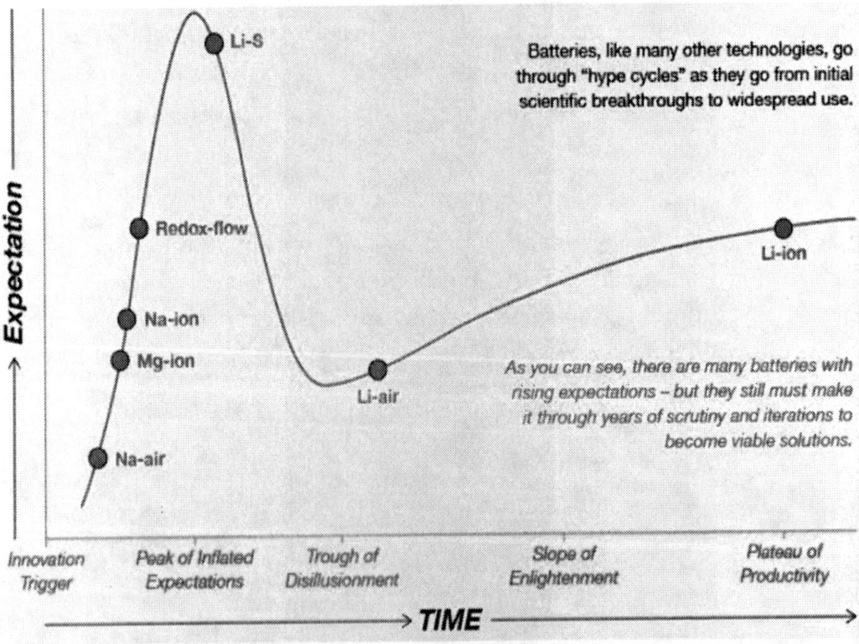

Figure 12: Source: visualcapitalist.com

Extending Lithium-ion in other ways

There are various ways in which researchers are exploring use of lithium-ions in other chemistries and methods. Some of these are summarized below:

Metal Air Batteries

Some time back, there was an impetus on using metal air batteries, which subsided as the technology could not emerge and LIBs made major stride. Recently, there has been a renaissance in development of this technology.

Aluminum Air Batteries

A new found focus on Aluminum–air batteries has emerged. The driver being that Al-air chemistry has one of the highest energy densities among all batteries. In the past, high anode cost and efficient byproduct removal was a challenge. An electric vehicle with Al-air battery can possibly achieve up to eight times the range of a LIB with a lower weight.

Al-air batteries are primary cells, i.e., non-rechargeable. The aluminum anode is consumed by reacting with atmospheric oxygen (cathode) immersed in a water-based electrolyte to form hydrated aluminum oxide, the battery will no longer produce electricity. Mechanically, it is possible to resurrect the battery with new aluminum anodes. These could be recycled from aluminum hydroxide that is produced.

Zinc Air Batteries

Zinc has emerged as a candidate for energy source for EVs. Zinc–air batteries have some properties of fuel cells as well as batteries: the zinc is the fuel, the reaction rate can be controlled by varying the air flow, and oxidized zinc/electrolyte paste can be replaced.

Zinc–air batteries and zinc–air fuel cells are powered by oxidizing zinc with oxygen from the air. They have high energy densities and are relatively inexpensive to produce to the size needed for EVs propulsion.

Lithium-Air

Anode: Lithium

Cathode: Porous carbon (Oxygen)

Promise: 10x greater energy density than Li-ion

Problems: Air is not pure enough and would need to be filtered. Lithium and oxygen form peroxide films that produce a barrier, ultimately killing storage capacity. Cycle life is only 50 cycles in lab tests.

Variations: Scientists also trying aluminum-air and sodium-air batteries as well.

Lithium-Sulphur

Anode: Lithium

Cathode: Sulphur, Carbon

Promise: Lighter, cheaper, and more powerful than li-ion

Problems: Volume expansion of up to 80%, causing mechanical stress. Unwanted reactions with electrolytes. Poor conductivity and poor stability at higher temperatures.

Variations: Many different variations exist, including using graphite/graphene, and silicon in the chemistry.

The first rechargeable zinc-air batteries were produced in 1996 to power vehicles using AC-based drive-trains. The vehicles that first used zinc-air batteries were small and mid-sized buses in Singapore. The advantage of using the zinc–air batteries for EV propulsion is that earth's supply of zinc is much more abundant than lithium. Research is on to see that zinc-air technology becomes commercialized.

Phinergy, an Israeli company, has developed innovative aluminum-air battery that is capable of providing energy to power an electric vehicle (EV) for up to 1000 miles at a time albeit, with stops every 200 miles to fill water (electrolyte). It claims to have developed technology of using nano-silver filters that prevent carbon dioxide from entering the system, which used to be a problem earlier resulting in carbonization of the anode. Each anodic plate holds energy to carry an EV for 20 miles and the system currently holds 50 of the plates at one time, which add up to a capacity of 1000 miles. Once the anodes are depleted they must be replaced. Recently, Indian companies like, Indian Oil Corporation and Ashok Leyland have entered into collaboration with Phinergy to commercialize this technology in India.

Flow Batteries

A flow battery based on redox (reduction–oxidation), is a type of electrochemical cell where chemical energy is provided by two chemical components dissolved in liquids contained within the system and separated by a membrane. Ion exchange occurs through the membrane while both liquids circulate in their own respective space. A flow battery may be used like a fuel cell or a rechargeable battery.

Recent research excitement to make flow batteries commercially viable is driven by issues around charging infrastructure of current LIBs. Such batteries have technical advantages over conventional rechargeable ones.

In flow batteries, separate liquid tanks (for anolyte and catholyte) can be mounted on the car itself (just like current gasoline tanks) and thereby unlimited longevity can be achieved. Electrolyte stored in this manner is usually pumped through the cells of the battery. They can be rapidly "recharged" by replacing the electrolyte liquid (in a similar way to refilling fuel tanks of IC engines) while simultaneously recovering the spent material for re-energization.

Various types of flow batteries have been developed, including redox, hybrid and membrane less. The fundamental difference between conventional batteries and flow cells is that energy is stored not as the electrode material in conventional batteries but as the electrolyte in flow cells.

Membrane less flow battery approach at Purdue University

A flow battery technology developed by Purdue researchers claim an "instantly rechargeable" method that is safe, affordable and environmentally friendly, akin to refueling a car at a petrol station.

Essentially, the technology uses, redox reactions in immiscible-fluids in porous media to achieve membrane less flow battery.

They claim to be the first to remove membranes from flow batteries leading to reduction in costs and extension of battery life. Membrane fouling can limit the number of recharge cycles and is a known contributor to many battery fires. Their startup called 'IF Battery' is producing components that are safe enough to be kept in a home garage and are stable enough to meet major production and distribution requirements in a cost effective manner.

MIT approach to develop an air-breathing flow battery

An MIT team has developed another kind of flow battery that breathes air, and can store energy long-term for about a fifth of the cost of existing technologies.

Their design of rechargeable flow battery uses anolyte which is made up of sulfur dissolved in water and they complemented it with a catholyte that is equally abundant (an oxygenated liquid salt solution). It turned out to be sodium which is a charge carrier to go back and forth between the sulfur and air electrode. In search for low cost positive electrode that could be used with sulfur cathode, they found out to be oxygen (air). The smart element of this battery is the fact that the catholyte "breathes" in air in from outside while discharging, and exhales while recharging. By this mechanism, the battery creates negatively-charged hydroxide ions in the catholyte while inhaling, and while recharging that oxygen is released, creating hydrogen ions which then send electrons back into the anolyte. Interestingly, unlike humans, this battery inhales and exhales oxygen and not carbon dioxide. This creates a charge balance by taking oxygen in and out of the system.

They believe that this battery would cost far less to make and run than lithium-ion batteries, while retaining almost the same energy density. Once in use, they estimate a scaled-up version of their flow battery would cost between US$20 and $30 per kWh stored to run, compared to about $100 per kWh for other storage systems.

Conclusion

The future of battery technology is very exciting, across the world in many research labs, the scientists are looking exciting breakthroughs. However, in the near and medium terms most of the research is focused on improving the already-commercialized lithium-ion.

How the battery market transforms itself in the next two decades, one does not know yet. However, one thing is certain that through human endeavor some of these technologies reviewed above may lead thc charge to a 100% renewable future.

CHAPTER FOUR

MAJOR COMPONENTS OF EVS: MOTORS, DRIVE TRAINS AND CONTROLLERS

Electric Vehicle do not have an Internal Combustion Engine (ICE) like a conventional vehicle instead it uses an electric motor to run the vehicle. Electric motors in EV's are usually powered by an onboard rechargeable battery. Electric vehicle also has lesser number of moving parts when compared to ICE (Precisely ICE has about 2000+ moving parts, while an EV has about 20 moving parts). Electric vehicles do not create any (or) negligibly less pollution than ICE powered vehicles, thus making it environmentally friendly (especially when used in cities).

The components of electric car are as follows:

Battery, electric motor and controller are the core components of any electric vehicle. Electric vehicle uses electric energy from battery to power the vehicle.

Electric Cars: Basic Principle

The "gas tank" for the electric vehicle is the battery. This battery acts as the power source and supplies electrical power to the electric motor which in turn moves and accelerates the vehicle. When the vehicle is idle it does not consume any energy as there is no electrical current flowing in the circuit. The motor unit is monitored and controlled by the controller, it acts as a regulator and controls the

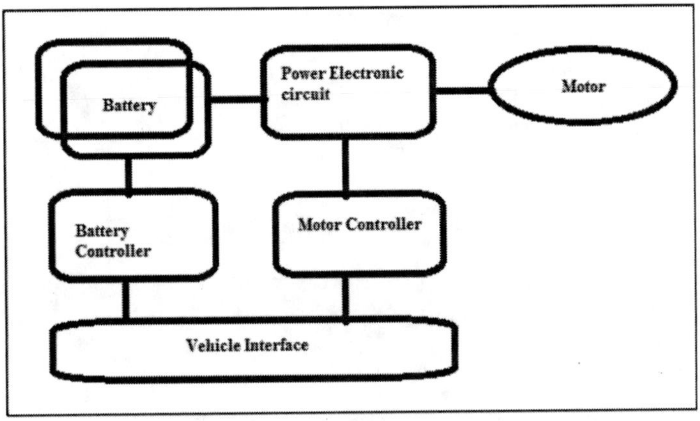

Figure 13: Basic components of Electric Vehicles

amount of power transferred to the motor form the battery so that the motor is saved from damages. All other electronic circuit and components receives power from the battery like any other internal combustion engine vehicle. The various other components of the car such as brakes, air conditioning, and airbags are similar to the normal conventional vehicle. As electric vehicle uses battery to power up the electrical motors the momentum of the motor can be used when the driver applies pressure on the brakes. When the brake is applied the electric motor behaves as an generator and charges the battery, when the power is cut from the motor the momentum of the motor generates electricity and feeds it back to recharge the batteries, unlike in normal fossil fuel cars potential energy in the motor is converted into heat. This process is known as regenerative braking.

Charging to driving process

Charging process is that where the electric batteries gets charged. It may be of internal or external type. In the internal charging process the charging takes place in regenerative braking process. In external process the battery gets charged by an external power source. Charging process can be subdivided into conductive charging and inductive charging. In conductive charging direct wires are connected to the car to charge whereas in inductive charging does

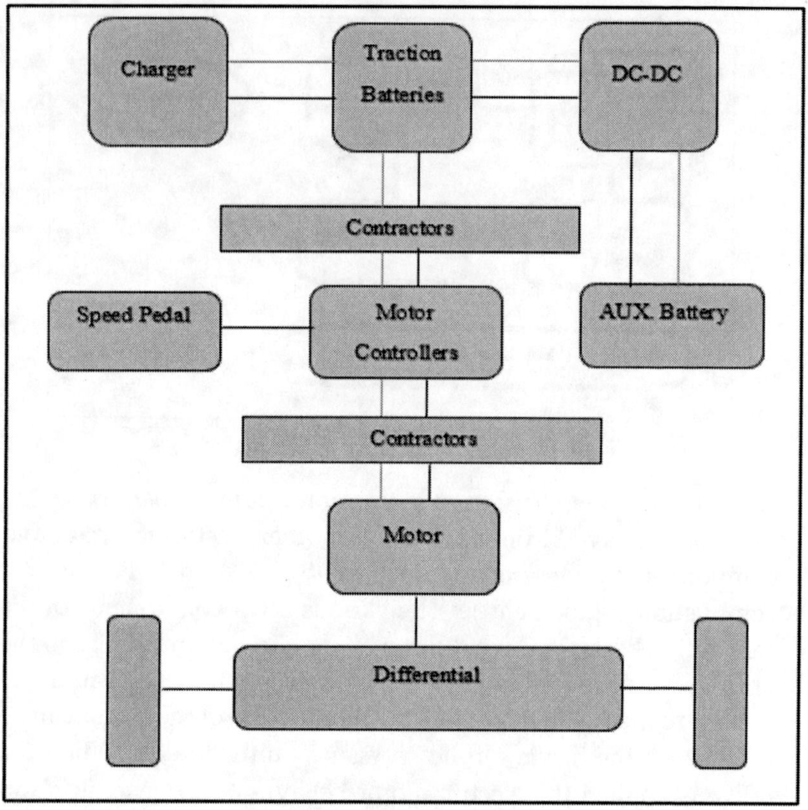

Figure 14: Working principles of electric cars

not require any wires, it is wireless transfer of powers. Conductive charging is of three types fast, medium and normal charging.

Electric motors used in electric vehicles

Internal Combustion Engines dominated the last century. It should be noted that there were lot of engine types in the past as well as in the present also. It would be much easier if we figure out the best engine so that we will end up having only one engine type. But the reality is different and there are numerous engine type such as flatheads, hemi, opposed, straight and V-configurations based upon the needs. The same scenario applies for EV's also. The old version of electric vehicles had lead acid batteries, DC brush motors and

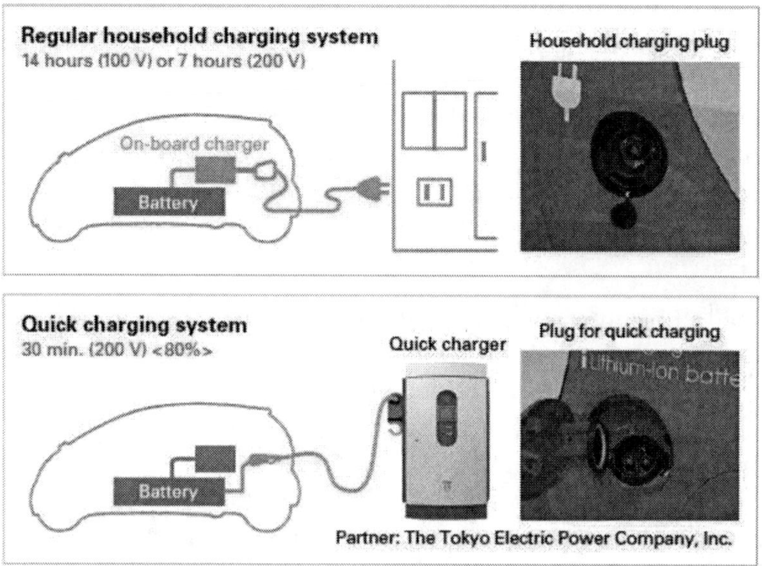

Figure 15: Household charging and quick charging

contactor controllers. But as technology progressed everything changed. Nowadays EV's use Li-ion battery instead of Lead acid batteries, DC brushless (or) induction motor instead of DC brush motor and modulating inverters instead of contractor controllers. The technology is still evolving and it is not sure whether the present configuration will stay or not. Apart from this different EV's uses different type of motor depending upon the application.

Operating Principles of Electric motor used in electric vehicles

The accelerator pedal in an electric vehicle is connected to a potentiometer which is also called as a variable resistance. This potentiometer is responsible for sending electric signal to the controller, which in turn will send power in the form of pulses from battery to motor. Let us consider if the pedal is not pressed at all. At this point of time, no electric signal is transferred to the controller so the motor does not work as. Similarly, if the pedal is pressed to the maximum, the maximum signal is sent to the controller which in turn transfers maximum power from the battery to the motor making it to delivers maximum power. It should be noted that Electric Vehicles are always fitted with 2 potentiometers for safety reasons. The controller compares the output of the two potentiometers in order to transfer power. In case if two potentiometer sends different signals then the controller will not transfer any power. If one potentiometer fails the other one acts as a reference.

Electric motor consists of two parts, stationary part called stator and rotating part called rotor as shown in Figure 17. Magnetic flux is created when electric current from battery flows through the windings of the stator. When current starts flowing in the stator core, magnetic flux is created on the current carrying conductors inserted on the core. This magnetic field induces current in the rotor, which in turn starts rotating as per Lenz law (Lenz law: the rotor will try to reduce every cause of producing current in it).

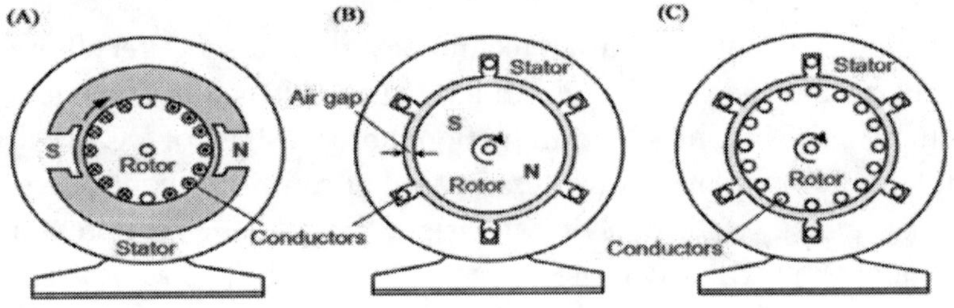

(A) DC Motor (B) AC Synchronous Motor and (C) AC Induction Motor

Figure 16: Configuration of Electric motor

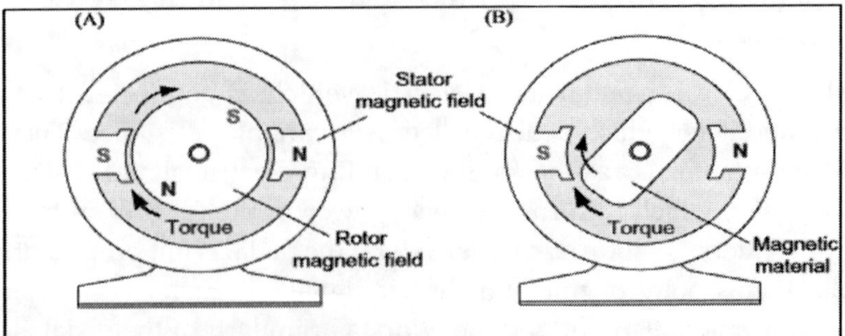

Rotation of electric motors. (A) Two magnetic fields and (B) one magnetic field and magnetic material.

Figure 17: Rotation of electric motors

Different types of motors used in electric vehicle

Motors used in electric vehicle is different when compared to stationary motors. The basic requirement for a motor to be used in electric vehicle is that it should produce propulsion torque over a various speed limit. Significant development in advanced control techniques and power electronics in recent years encouraged automobile manufacturers to use different kind of motors in electric vehicles depending upon their application. Important parameters for a motor to be used in Electric Vehicle are:

1. Good Efficiency
2. High Starting Torque
3. High Power Density

Both AC and DC motors are used in electric vehicles. Commonly used motors in electric vehicle are:

1. DC Series Motor
2. Brushless DC Motor (BLDC)
3. Permanent Magnet Synchronous Motor (PMSM)
4. Three phase AC Induction Motor
5. Switched Reluctance Motor

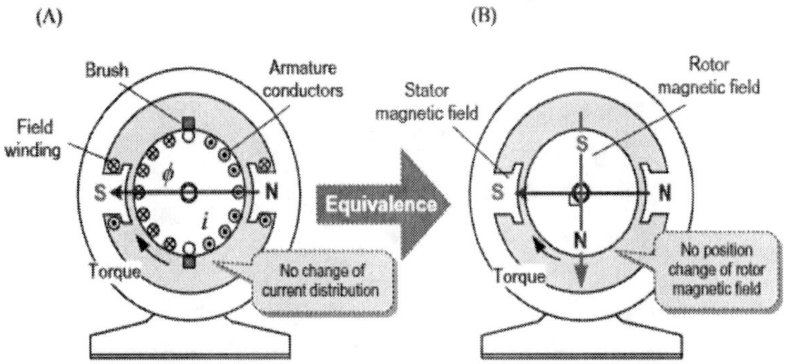

Operating principle of the DC motor. (A) Rotor current and stator magnetic field and (B) two magnetic fields.

Figure 18: Operating Principles of DC Motors

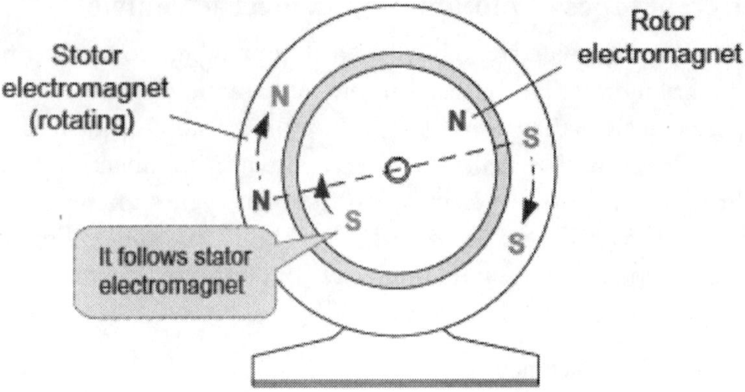

Figure 19: Operating Principles of AC motor

DC Series Motor

DC series motor falls under the category of DC brushed motors. These motors were used in electric vehicles during early stages. The main advantage of this motor is that it provides higher torque than any other motor earning it a name "King of electric car motor". Because of its disadvantages such as heat generation at brushes, bulky structure, lower efficiency and poor battery utilization these motors have phased out from electric vehicles. They were mostly used in first-generation electric vehicles.

Used in: Fiat Panda Electric, Conceptor G-Van

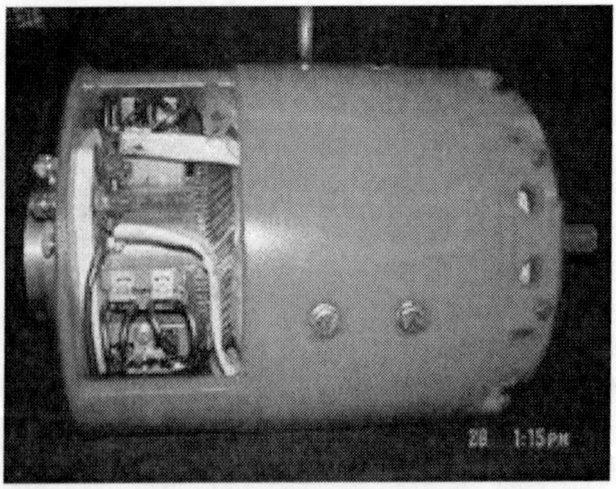

Figure 20: DC motor cutaway windings

Brushless DC Motor (BLDC)

BLDC motors are similar to DC permanent magnet motors. This motor does not have brush and commutator arrangement as in DC brushed motor. Here the commutation is done electronically and hence these motors are maintenance free. The main advantages of these motors are: high starting torque, high efficiency, high specific power density, no rotor copper loss. There are two types of BLDC motors:

1. Out runner type BLDC motor
2. In-runner type BLDC motor

Out runner type BLDC motor:

This type of BLDC motor has a unique arrangement (i.e.) the stator is present inside and the rotor is present outside. This type of motor generally does not require any gear system and some motors comes with inbuilt planetary gear system. This motor is called Hub Motor because the exterior rotor is directly connected to the wheels. The main advantages of this motor are that it is less bulky as it requires no gear system and it has less maintenance.

Used in: Hulikkal e-bike, Tronx t-bike, Spero e-bike, 22 Kymco electric scooter.

In-runner type BLDC motor:

In-runner motor arrangement is similar to a normal conventional motor (i.e.) rotor is present inside and stator is present outside. Due to this arrangement In-runner type BLDC motor requires an extra transmission arrangement making it bulky when compared to out-runner BLDC motor. This motor is widely used in 3-wheelers and in some low as well as medium performance level scooters also.

Used in: Kinetic Green, Volta Automotive Autos, Ather 450 scooter.

Figure 21: BLDC motor used in Ather 450

BLDC motors are widely used for 2-wheeler and 3-wheeler type electric vehicle. Even though these motors are widely used they are expensive. The escalation in costs is due to the presence of permanent magnet and overloading this motor will eventually damage the permanent magnets.

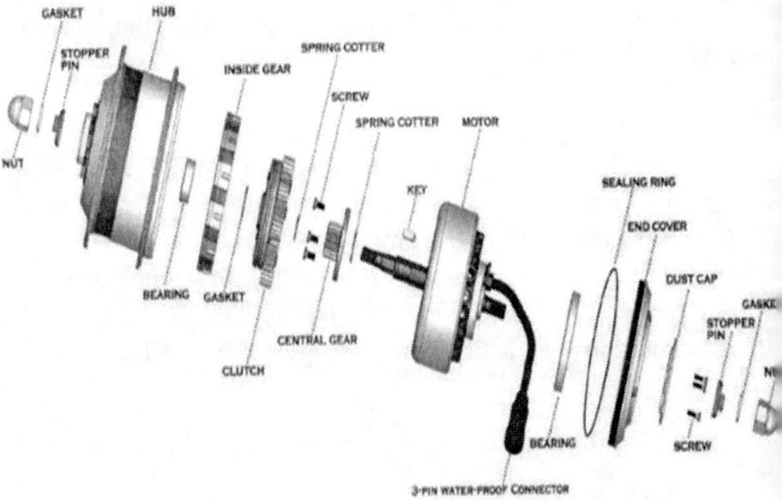

Figure 22: Cross sectional view of BLDC motor

Permanent Magnet Synchronous Motor

Permanent Magnet Synchronous Motor (PMSM) is similar to permanent magent BLDC motor with same characteristics like higher efficiency and high power density. The main advantages of permanent magnet synchronous motors are: It can produce high torque even at low speed, compact, capable of operating in different speeds without any gear system. PMSM is more costlier when compared to both induction motor and BLDC motor. However PMSM is giving stiffcompetition to induction motor as the former is more efficient than the latter. PMSM is the best option for high performance cars and buses. The main difference between PMSM and BLDC is that BLDC has trapezoidal back EMF and PMSM has sinusoidal back EMF.

The main disadvantages of PMSM are: It experience more iron loss while operated at high speed during in-wheel mode of operation, expensive when compared to induction motors due to the presence of permanent magnets.

Used in: Nissan Leaf, Kia Soul, Toyota Prius.

Figure 23: Chevrolet Bolt's permanent magnet electric motor

3-Phase AC induction motors

This is the third most popular motor used in electric car. This motor uses the similar batteries as a DC motor does, for power source. Since the power is provided by batteries is DC, an inverter is used in the place of the controller, to convert DC into 3-phase AC. The induction motor will not produce high torque under fixed voltage and fixed frequency unlike a DC motor, but it can be done with the help of advanced control techniques such as FOC or v/f method. The main advantages of the motor are: Simple and rugged construction and can operate in complex environment, less expensive because of the absence of brushes, commutators and slip rings, less maintenance, can be operated in explosive environment.

Complex controller and inverter circuit adds up the price of whole setup which is the major disadvantage of using 3-phase AC induction in electric vehicle.

Used in: Tesla Model X, Tesla Model S, General Motors EV1, Toyota RAV4.

Figure 24: 3-phase AC Induction motor

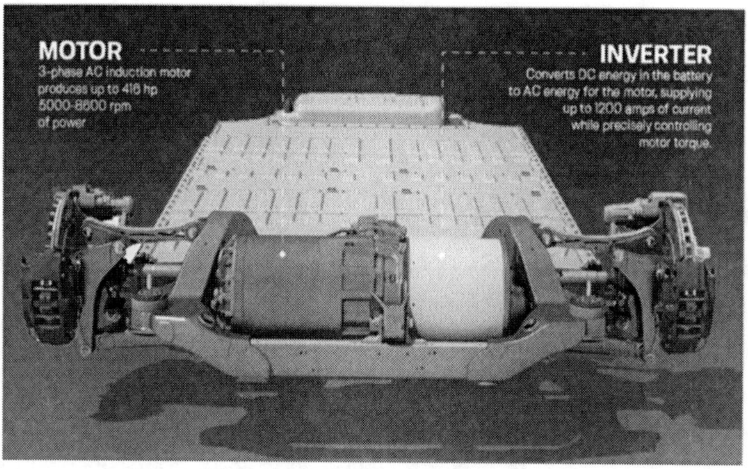

Figure 25: Induction motor in an EV powertrain

Motors used in EVs

There is a variety of Electric motor out there, but a few only make up the majority of motor being used in EV:

1. The Series wound DC motor
2. The Permanent magnet motor
3. The 3- phase AC motor.

Table 1: List of Motors with Specifications

Motors	*Specification*	*Model*	*Price*	*Manufacturer*
	200KW Dual Siemens Azure AC Induction 3 Phase Motor 1PV5135 4WS14		$8,995.00	Siemens
	AM Racing AMR 250-90 Single AC Motor - Liquid Cooled, Permanent Magnet - Remy Cartridge	AMR 250-90	$9,288.00	AM Racing
	AM Racing AMR Dual Stack 250-90 AC Motor - Liquid Cooled, Permanent Magnet – Remy	AMR 250-90D	$18,488	AM Racing

Motors	Specification	Model	Price	Manufacturer
	Curtis 1236SE-5621 HPEVS AC-20 Brushless AC Motor Kit - 48 Volt	AC20/48	$2,730.00	HPEVS
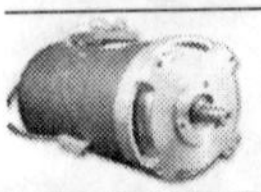	Curtis 1236SE-5621 HPEVS AC-34 Brushless AC Motor Kit - 48 Volts	AC-34-48	$2,960.0	HPEVS
	Curtis 1236SE-5621 HPEVS AC-9 Brushless AC Motor Kit - 48 Volt	Motor	$2,460.00	HPEVS
	Curtis 1238-6501 HPEVS AC-12 Brushless AC Motor Kit - 72 Volt	Motor	$2,960.0	HPEVS
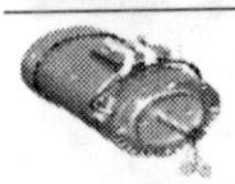	Curtis 1238-6501 HPEVS AC-20 Brushless AC Motor Kit - 72 Volt	Motor	$3,000.00	HPEVS
	Curtis 1238-6501 HPEVS AC-34 Brushless AC Motor Kit - 72 Volt	Motor	$3,480.0	HPEVS
	Curtis 1238-7601 HPEVS AC-15 Brushless AC Motor Kit - 96 Volt	Motor	$3,120.0	HPEVS
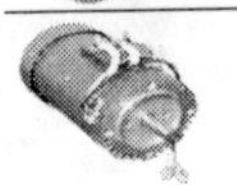	Curtis 1238-7601 HPEVS AC-20 Brushless AC Motor Kit - 96 Volt	Motor	$3,375.0	HPEVS
	Curtis 1238-7601 HPEVS AC-20 Brushless AC Motor Kit - 96 Volt	Motor	$3,375.0	HPEVS

Parameters of electric motor used in EVs

Power to weight ratio

Power to weight ratio is usually calculated to find the performance of a motor as a whole. It is calculated by dividing the entire output power by the mass (weight) of the motor to arrive at a metric which is not dependent on motor size.

Power to weight ratio of motor can be given by:

$$\text{Power to weight ratio } \frac{\text{Peak power of motor in kW}}{\text{Weight of motor in kg}} \quad (1)$$

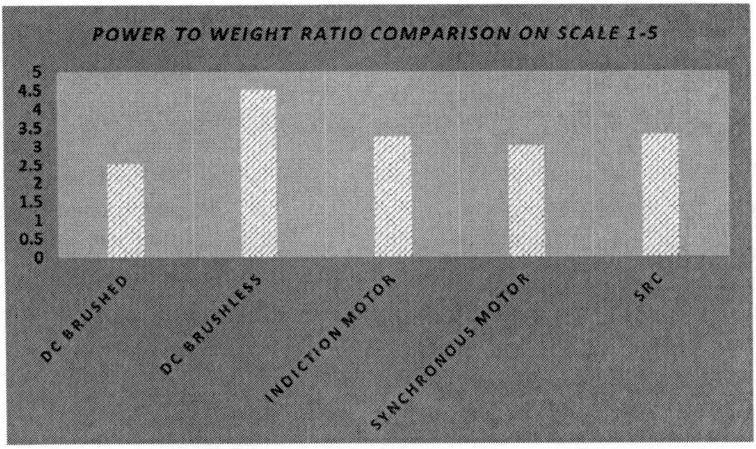

Figure 26: Peak power to weight ratio comparison

Figure 26 shows peak power to weight ratio comparison for different electric motors used in EVs. Motor with a higher peak power to weight ratio is always more suitable for electric vehicles. BLDC and Induction motor have high power to weight ratio, so they are used mostly in electric vehicles.

Torque speed characteristic of induction machine

Torque speed characteristic of IM in motor and generator operation mode are shown in figure 27. Induction machine in generator mode has better torque speed characteristic.

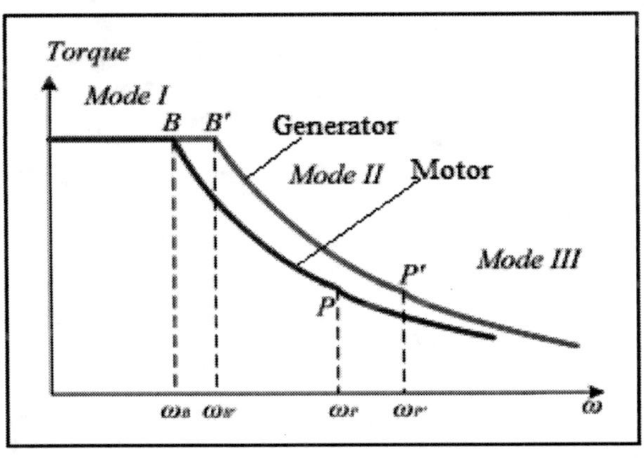

Figure 27: Torque-speed characteristic of induction machine

Performance & applicability of motor for electric vehicle can be declared by using the torque speed characteristics.

Effect of stator resistance on torque – speed characteristic

Torque/Electromagnetic power characteristic of IM at different stator resistance are shown in Figs. 28 & 29. For a given speed, IM's generator working mode has high torque carrying capacity at higher value of stator resistance.

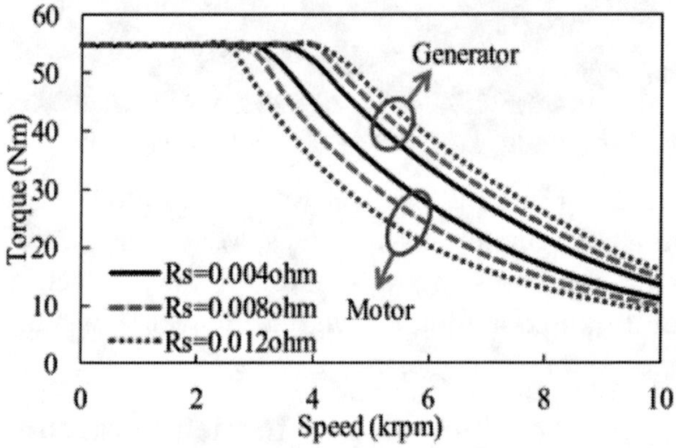

Figure 28: Torque speed characteristic of IM at different stator resistance

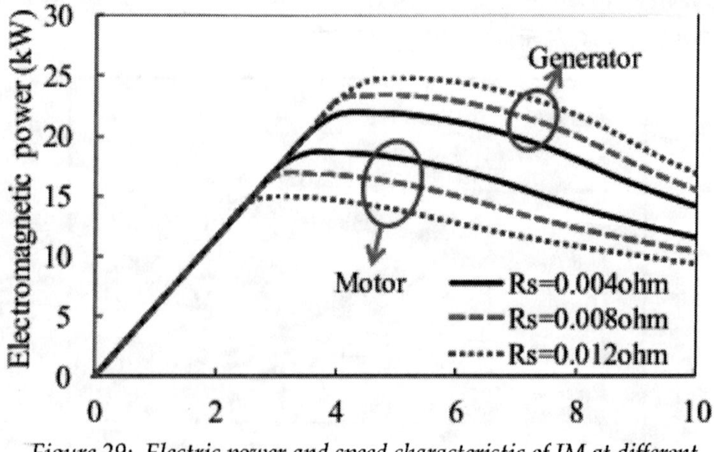

Figure 29: Electric power and speed characteristic of IM at different stator resistance

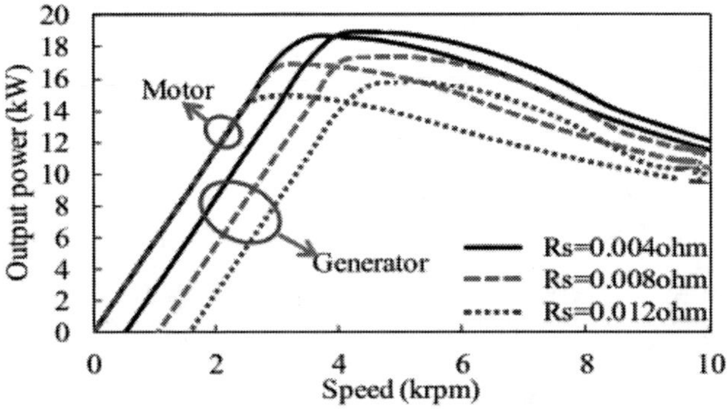

Figure 30: Output power and speed characteristic of IM in different modes

Despite the fact that the distinction of electromagnetic power between the engine and generator activity modes in the motion debilitating area increments with Rs the distinction of yield control does not change clearly, as shown in Figure 30.

Torque speed characteristic of different motors

DC series wound motor has a starting torque in addition speed decreases with increase in torque as shown in Figure 31. DC shunt motor have medium starting torque motor, but speed decreases slightly with increase in torque as there in Figure 32. DC shunt wound motors are usually used in constant speed application. Torque-speed characteristics of brushless DC motor is more drooping than that of DC shunt motor. Torque-speed characteristics of an induction motor slightly differ with different values of rotor resistance. Presence of breakdown torque, constant power operation is limited in induction motor. Figure 33.

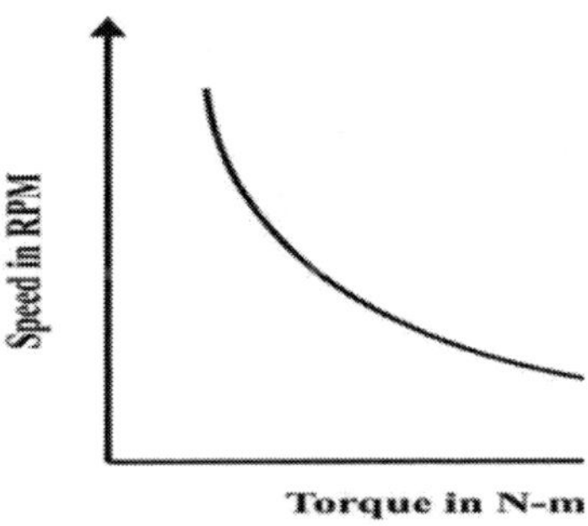

Figure 31: Torque speed characteristic of DC series wound Motor

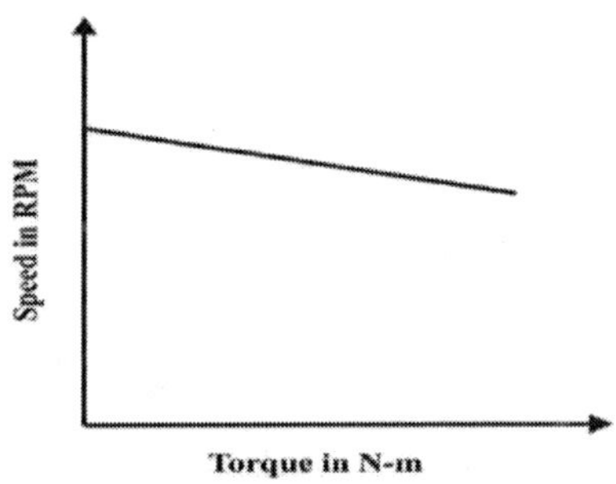

Figure 32: Torque speed characteristic of DC shunt wound motor

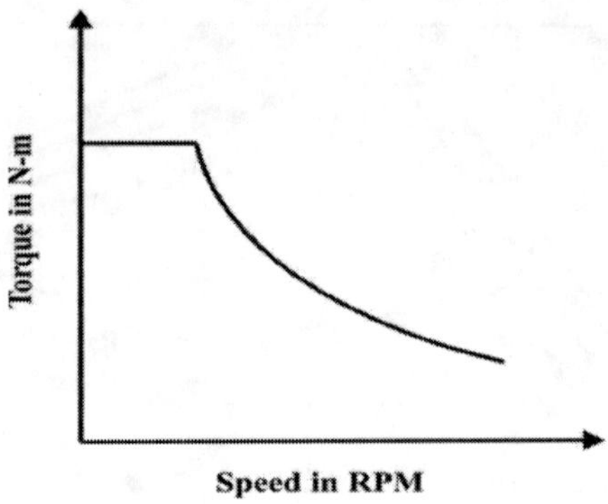

Figure 33: Torque speed characteristic of Switched Reluctance motor

Efficiency comparison

Electrical efficiency of motor gives the relationship between electrical inputs and useful mechanical output of motor and is generally given by ratio of shaft power output & motor input power.

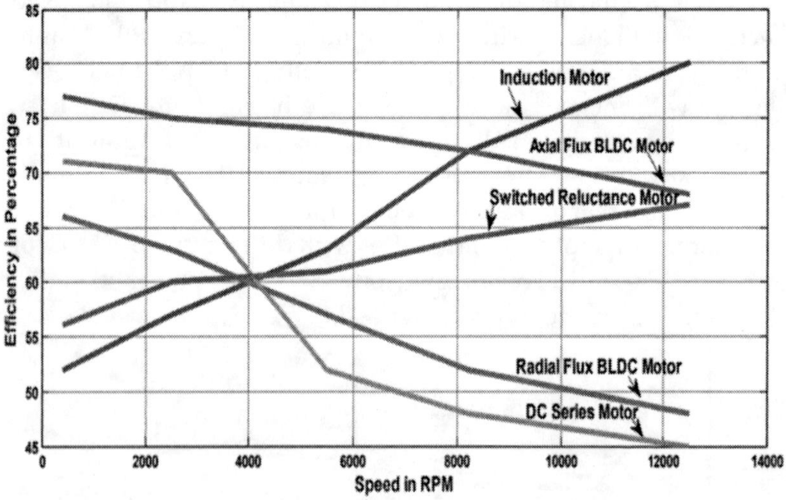

Figure 34: Relation between speed and efficiency of different motors used in EV's

Table 2: Efficiency Comparison

Motor Type	*Peak Efficiency*	*Efficiency at 10% load*
DC brushed Motor	85-90	80-85
DC brushless Motor	> 95	70-80
AC Induction Motor	> 90	> 90
Synchronous Motor	> 92	80-85
Switched Reluctance Motor	< 95	> 90

Cost of motor comparison

Price of different electric motors with same rated voltage and output power ratings is compared as shown in Figure 34A. The most important challenges ahead for EV manufacturers is to provide consumer with an EV as good as gasoline vehicles but in an affordable price.

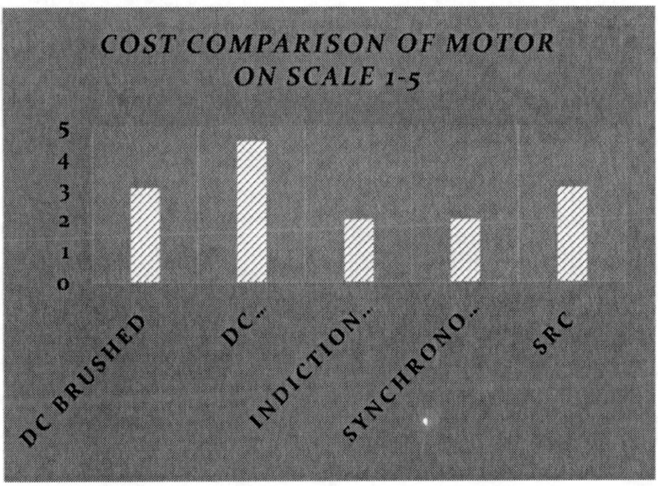

Figure 34A: Cost comparison of Motor

Drivetrain system

Control system of Electric Vehicles include five electric control units (ECUs),

1. Main ECU,
2. Motor ECU,

3. Battery ECU,
4. Brake ECU, and
5. Electric Equipment ECU.

The main ECU controls the motor torque by computing based on the information such as the car speed and the accelerator position, resulting in the drive torque of electric vehicle.

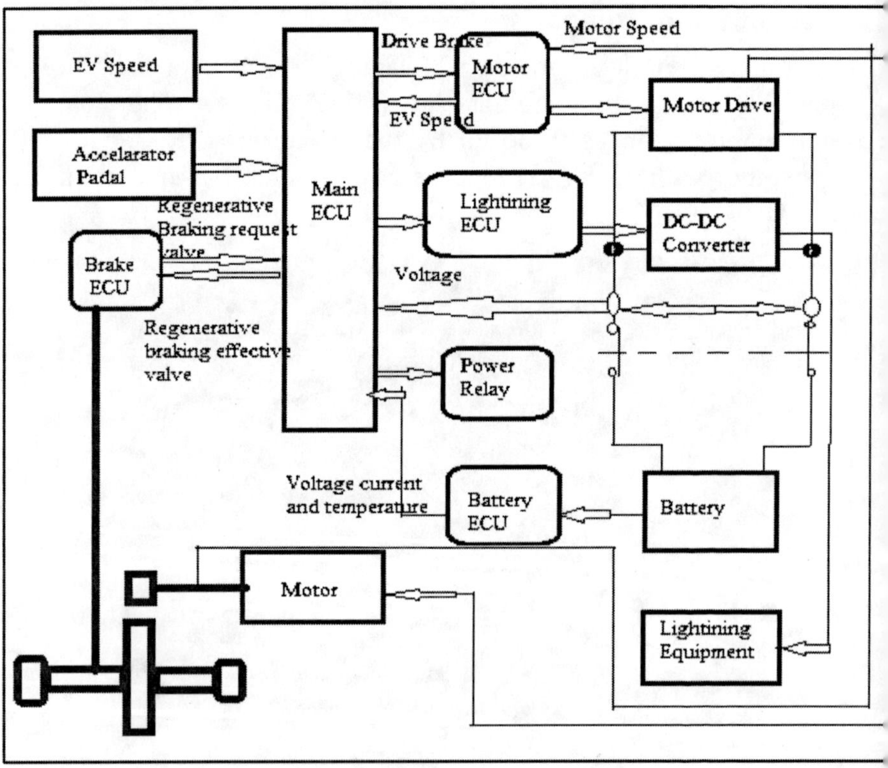

Figure 35: Control Schematic of EVs

The torque-speed characteristic, power weight ratio, cost and drive train are major factors influencing the selection of the Motor of Electric Vehicles. Figure 35 shows the drive train of an electric vehicles including different ECUs and Figure.36 shows the drive train of an internal combustion engine.

Engine → Clutch → Transmission → Differential Gear → Wheet

Figure 36: Drive train of IC engine

Electric Vehicle drive train system

Conventional type

Conventional type of drive train system has engine replaced with the electric motor, rest of the structure of the drivetrain basically remain same, as shown in Figure 37.

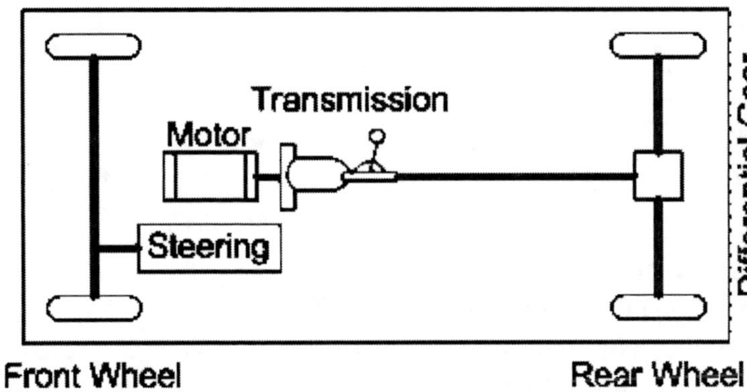

Figure 37: Conventional drive train system

Transmission less type

The simplified form of the conventional drive train is the transmission less type where the transmission is removed from the drivetrain system as shown in Fig. 38.

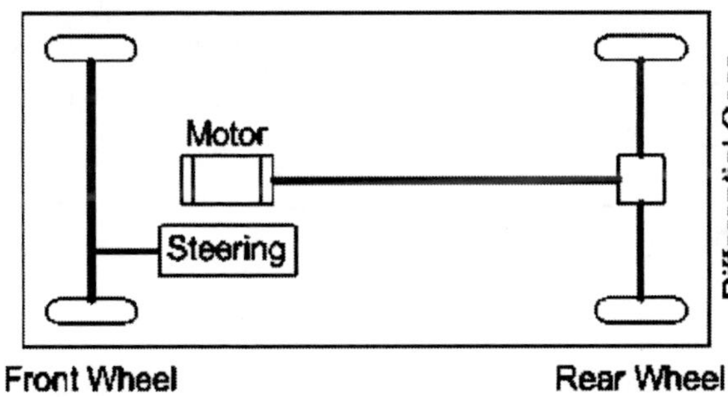

Figure 38: Transmission less drive train system

Cascade Type

In cascade drive system, two motors are attached on wheel side to provide and transmit torque and differentials are removed, as shown in Fig. 39, is the simplest type of transmission system.

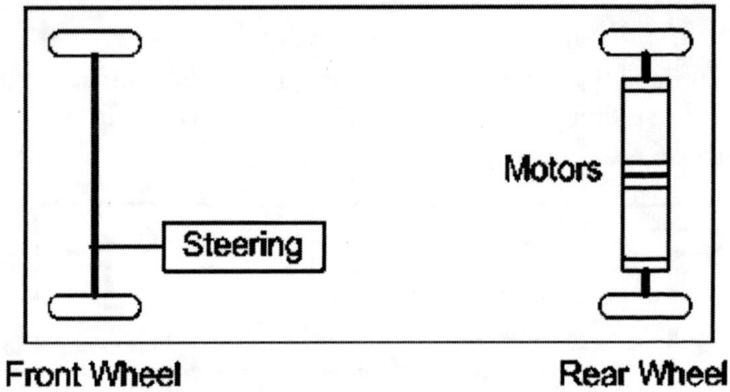

Figure 39: Cascade type drive train system

In wheel type with reduction gear

In wheel type of drive system, two motors are directly fixed to the wheel side with reduction gear provided to drive the wheel at ambient torque and speed as shown in Figure 40.

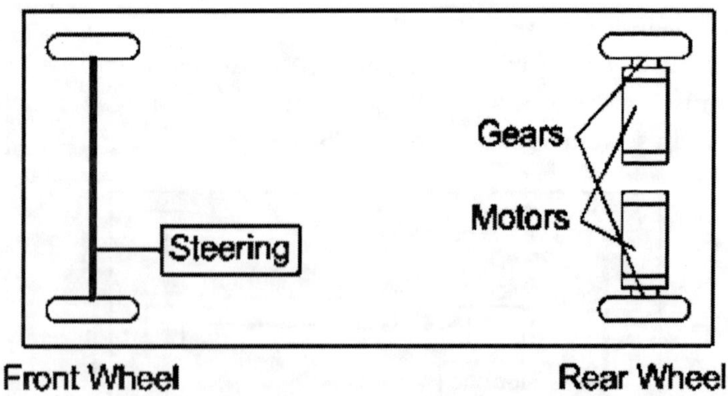

Figure 40: In wheel type with reduction gear

In wheel direct drive type

In wheel direct drive type or the direct-drive type of in-wheel drivetrain system, rear wheels and motors are integrated so that rotations can be caused directly without resort to gear, as shown in Figure 41.

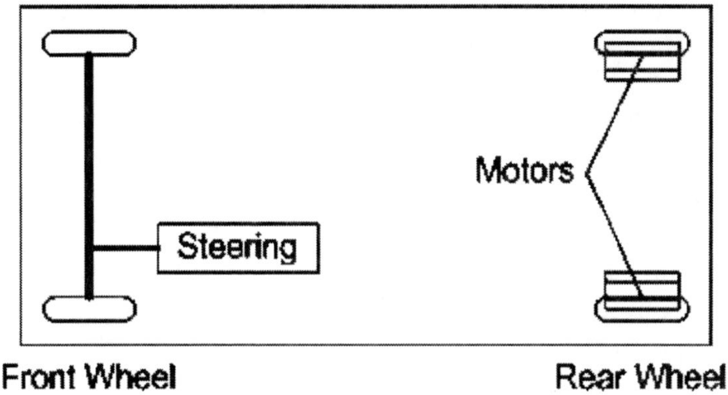

Figure 41: In wheel type direct drive type

Four-wheel direct type

In this type of system, four in-wheel motors are used to directly drive four wheels, to control the direction of the EV an electric steering is used, as shown in Figure 42.

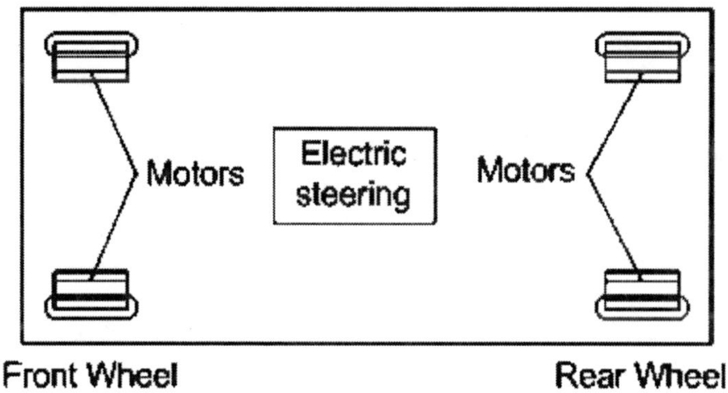

Figure 42: Four wheel direct type

Transmission for Electric Vehicle

Conventional thinking on EV drivelines are used for single-speed transmission, relying on torque spread of electric motor to provide adequate performance under all operating conditions. Though simple to execute. This arrangement cannot achieve high efficiency because, for much of time, the traction motor is operating at loads & speeds that don't yield optimum efficiency.

Electric Dual Clutch Transmission (eDCT)

The eDCT (electric Dual Clutch Transmission) takes into consideration a sum of seven apparatus blends from the four unmistakable rigging proportions through a mix of single-engine driving (in the first place, second, third and fourth apparatus) and double engine driving mixes (first and second, second and third, third and fourth rigging).

Replacing clutches with motors

The transmission concept of eDCT from Oerlikon Graziano is based on dual clutch transmission (DCT) principle, providing seamless shifting between ratios without torque interruption, using no clutches or synchronizers. Configuration is similar to DCT but use 2 motor in place of twin clutches. One motor drives a shaft carrying first and third gears (the "odd" shaft) and the other drives a shaft carrying second and fourth (the "even" shaft). This permits pre-determination of the following rigging before the past one has been separated, utilizing the two engines to synchronize shaft speeds with the goal that no synchronizers are required.

Figures 43 & 44 class car application uses electromechanical shift actuation, via an electric Motor and barrel cam, and an open differential.

Figure 43: Transmission with opposed motor arrangement

Figure 44: Transmission with parallel motor arrangement

Controllers

The controller will deliver a controlled voltage to motor, which will be depending upon potentiometer output and pulse width modulation controlling speed. Controllers can be described as two types:

1. DC controller; and 2. AC Controller

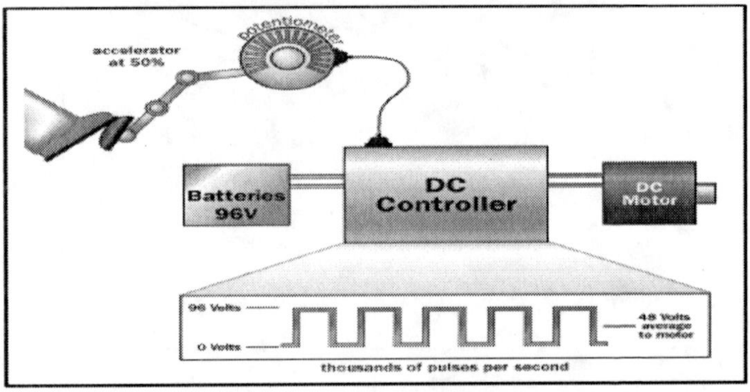

Figure 45: DC Controllers

A DC controller connects batteries with DC motor. If driver floors the accelerate pedal, controller will provide full 95V from batteries to motor, while 0V while the drive pulls away the foot from pedal. For any sitting in between, the controller "chops" this 96V a thousands of times/second to create an average voltage between 0 and 96V.

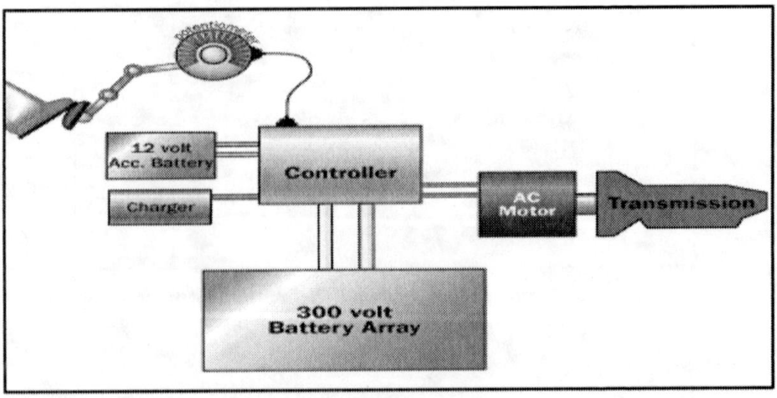

Figure 46: AC Controllers

An AC controller snares to an AC engine. Utilizing six arrangements of energy transistors, the controller takes in 300 volts DC and produces 240 volts AC, 3-stage. The controller also gives a charging framework to the batteries, and a DC-to-DC converter to revive the 12-volt embellishment battery.

In Fig. 46, the controller takes in 300 volts DC from the battery pack. It changes over it into a most extreme of 240 volts AC, three-stage, to send to the engine. It does these utilizing huge transistors that quickly turn the batteries' voltage on and off to make a sine wave. When we push on the gas pedal, a link from the pedal interfaces with these two potentiometers.

Figure 47: The 300-volt, 50-kilowatt controller for this electric car is the box marked "U.S. Electricar"

The flag from the potentiometers (Figure 47) advises the controller how much energy to convey to the electric auto's engine. There are two potentiometers for security's purpose. The controller peruses the two potentiometers and ensures that their signs are equivalent. In the event that they are not, at that point the controller does not work. This game plan makes preparations for a circumstance where a potentiometer flops in the all-out position.

Figure 48: The potentiometers hook to the gas pedal and send a signal to the controller.

The controller's work to DC electric car is easy. Assuming battery pack contains 12V batteries, series wired creating 144V. The controller takes 144V DC, Delivering it to motor in a controlled manner.

The most straightforward DC controller would be an enthusiastic about/off change wired to the quickening agent pedal. When we push the pedal, it would turn the switch on, and when we take your foot off the pedal, it would turn it off. As the driver, you would need to push and discharge the quickening agent to beat the engine on and off to keep up a given speed.

Clearly, that kind of on/off approach would work yet it would be a torment to drive, so the controller does the beating for you. The controller peruses the setting of the quickening agent pedal from the potentiometers and directs the power likewise. Give us a chance to state that we have the quickening agent drove mostly down. The controller peruses that setting from the potentiometer and quickly changes the ability to the engine on and off with the goal that it is on a fraction of the time and off a fraction of the time. In the event that we have the quickening agent pedal 25 percent of the route down, the controller beats the power so it is on 25 percent of the time and off 75 percent of the time.

Figure 49: Heavy cables connect the battery pack to controller

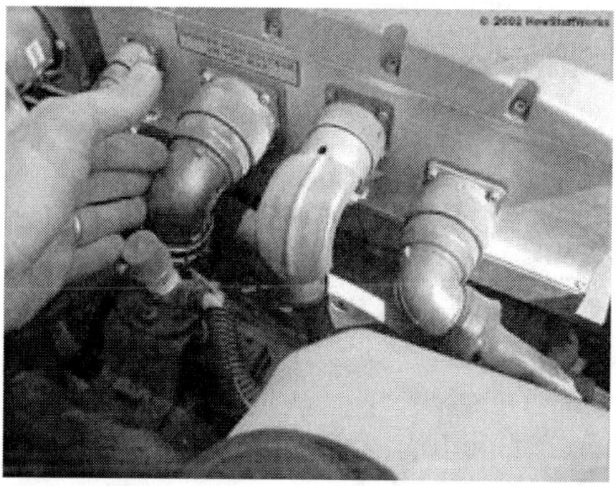

Figure 50: The heavy wires entering and leaving the controller

AC controller's job is little bit complicated, but it's the same idea. The controller creates 3 pseudo-sine waves. It does this by taking the DC voltage from the batteries and beating it on and off. In an AC controller, there is the extra need to switch the extremity of the voltage 60 times each second. In this manner, you really require six arrangements of transistors in an AC controller, while you require just a single set in a DC controller. In the AC controller, for each stage you require one arrangement of transistors to beat the voltage and another set to turn around the extremity. You imitate that three times for the three stages - six aggregate arrangements of transistors.

Regenerative Braking System (RBS)

Introduction

In conventional braking system a part of kinetic energy is lost in braking due to friction & carried away by stream of air. In Regenerative breaking (Figure 51) some part of kinetic energy is stored during deceleration. The energy can be stored in form of pressure in hydraulic cylinder & can be transmitted whenever required. This should be possible by utilizing a removal pump-to-direct water powered liquid into a collector. The collector can discharge the weight when there is speeding up and this outcome in increment in effectiveness.

A regenerative braking system, as shown in Figure 51, should ideally have the following properties:

1. Effective energy conversion.
2. Energy storing have high capacity per unit weight and volume.
3. High power rating so large amount of energy can flow in a short space of time
4. Not require over complicated system to link it with the vehicle transmission
5. Smooth delivery of power from the regenerative system
6. Absorb the store braking energy in direct proportion to braking

Working Principle of RBS

Regenerative braking system consist of drive modes and Braking modes. In drive, mode energy of motor is used to drive flywheel and in braking mode, part of the kinetic energy is stored in battery or accumulator.

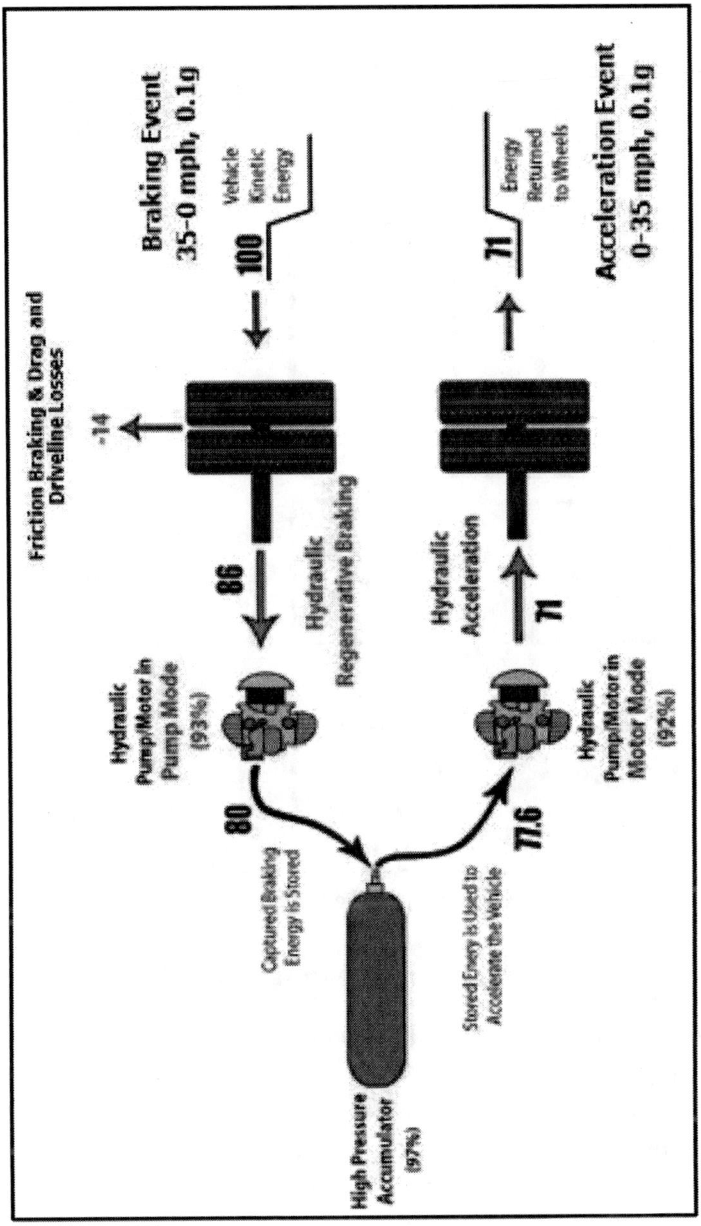

Figure 51: Regenerative Braking System

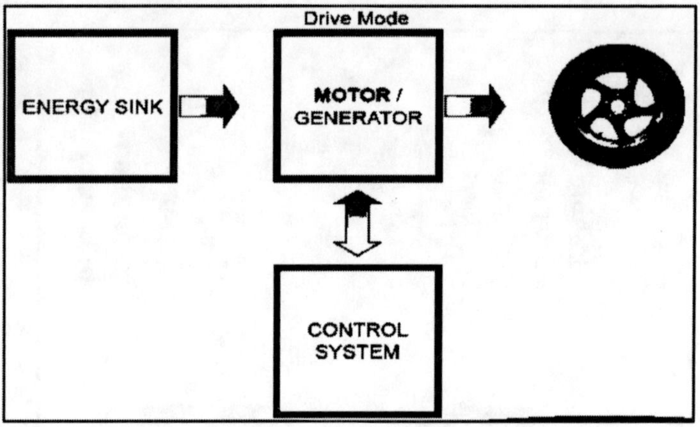

Figure 52: Regenerative braking system: Drive mode

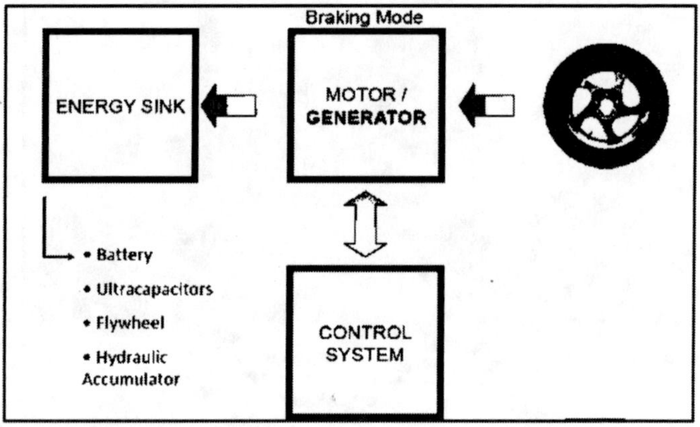

Figure 53: Regenerative Braking system: Braking mode

Different types of regenerative braking system

Electric regenerative braking system

Electric driven framework comprises of electric engine, which go about as generator and engine both. In such kinds of framework, amid increasing speed electric engine drives vitality from battery to give additional main impetus to move the vehicle and amid braking electric supply from battery is cutoff.

Hydraulic regenerative braking system

In HRBS burring braking reversible pump sends water powered liquid from low weight aggregator inside the vehicle into a high weight gatherer and this moderates the vehicle. The liquid stays under strain in the collector until the point when the driver pushes the cylinder once more.

Challenges and Future

- Battery Problems
    1. Long recharging time – refueling required only minutes.
    2. Battery weight – 100-pound Lead acid batteries = 1 pound of gasoline.
    3. Battery costs.
    4. Lithium would be imported from China- Like Crude Oil is done.
- Range concerns
- Price
- Consumer acceptance
- Market

CHAPTER FIVE

TYPES OF CHARGERS FOR ELECTRIC VEHICLES

Introduction

Not all electric car are built the same. EVs are available in a variety of models with different ranges and capabilities. To recharge, they are plugged in to a source of electric power through Electric Vehicle Supply Equipment (EVSE). *It is the intermediary between a power source and the vehicle's charging port, and is typically mounted on a wall or up on a pedestal. Its role is to simply relay the AC power to the vehicle safely.* The maximum rate at which the EV battery can be refilled depends on the capacity of the charger in the vehicle and amount of power the EVSE can supply.

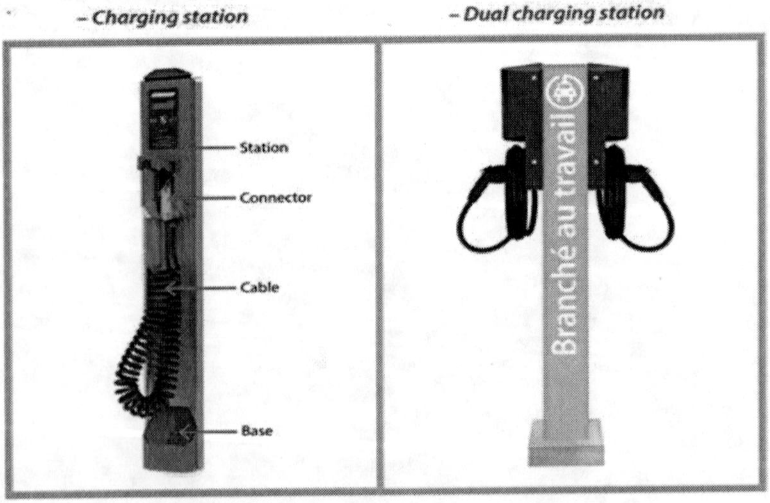

Figure 54: EV Charging Station, Source: Google

Different Types of EV Chargers

At the first sight, charging an electric car seems to be a simple process, implying that one can plug one's car into a charger that is connected to the electric grid. However, it is not as simple. It depends on the types of EVSE that one has deployed. In some cases, specially, in personal garages one connects the cable on one end to a domestic power socket and the other end to the car's charging port. However, many more sophisticated design have emerged which will be reviewed in this chapter.

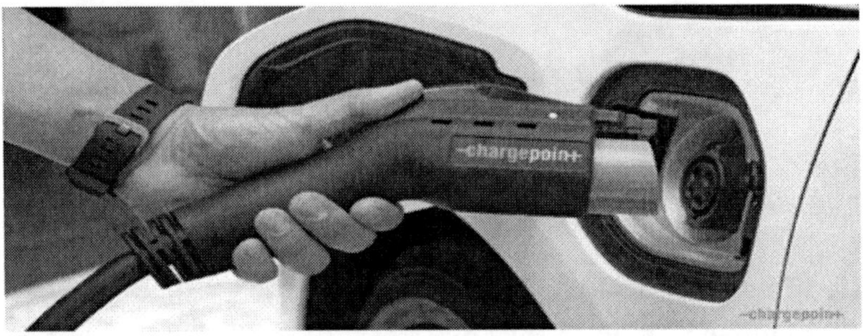

EV chargers typically fall under one of three main categories: Level 1 charging stations, Level 2 charging stations, and DC Fast Chargers (also referred to as Level 3 charging stations).

Table 3: Different Types of Charging

	Level 1	Level 2	Fast charge
Voltage	120 V	208 or 240 V	200 to 450 V
Current type	AC	AC	DC
Useful power	1.4 kW	7.2 kW	50 kW
Maximum output	1.9 kW	19.2 kW	150 kW
Charging time[a]	12 h[a]	3 h[a]	20 min[b]
Connector	J1772	J1772	J1772 Combo, CHAdeMO and Supercharger

a. Charging time of a completely discharged 16-kWh battery at useful power.

b. Charging time to 80% charge, i.e., 12 kWh. Fast charging cannot be sustained to a full charge.

Source: SAE.

As we see, from the table 3, some chargers are faster than others.

And, not only this, but we must also realize that different electric cars need different types of charging ports.

SAE J1772	Type 2 (Mennekes)
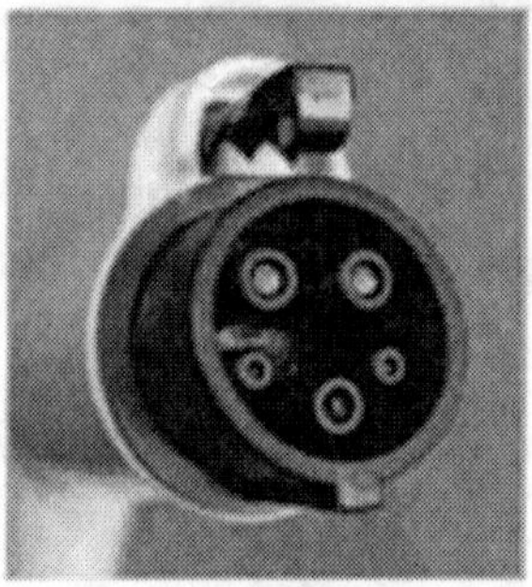	
North America and Japan	Europe and China

Figure 55: Types of Charging Ports

This brings us to the concept of **On-board charger.** The actual charging device for Level 1 and Level 2 charging comes factory-installed in the car and is called the "on-board charger." It converts AC power from the wall to DC power that charges the battery in the vehicle. The charging speed may vary, but the most common on-board chargers are 6.6 kW on battery electric vehicles (BEVs) and 3.3 kW on plug-in hybrid electric vehicles (PHEVs). As shown in the figure above, the connector styles are also different depending on the type of "OBC".

Level 1 Chargers

Level 1 chargers simply use a plug to connect to the on-board charger and a standard household (120v) outlet and are typically used in North America. These are the slowest chargers. However, unlike other chargers, Level 1 chargers do not require the installation of any additional equipment and are popular for residential use. They are the least expensive EVSE option. While this option may not look great, it works for those commuters who travel less than 40 miles a day and have all night to charge. Some popular manufacturers of Level 1 EV chargers include AeroVironment, Duosida, Leviton, and Orion.

Level 2 Chargers

These chargers must use an EVSE to provide power at 220v or 240v and up to 30 amps. Level 2 chargers are used by both residential and commercial charging stations. They, however cannot be plugged into a standard wall outlet and require professional installation. Such chargers can fully charge an electric car battery within two hours. This makes them an ideal option for commuters who need fast charging and businesses who want to offer charging stations to consumers as a perquisite while they shop, bank, or have a meal. The popular Level 2 chargers manufacturers include ClipperCreek, Chargepoint, JuiceBox, and Siemens. Many electric car manufacturers, like Nissan, have their own Level 2 charger products. Currently, effort is on to improve charging capacity of these chargers to further reduce the charging time.

Level 3 or DC Fast Charging

Since most users of EV wanted faster charging in lesser time, the fast charging DC chargers emerged. Initially, Japanese took the lead as they had the cars ready viz, Nissan Leaf and Mitsubishi i-MiEV. They developed the chargers known as CHAdeMO EV charging stations. There is an interesting story behind this name. According to Wikipedia, *CHAdeMO is an abbreviation of "CHArge de MOve", equivalent to "move using charge" or "move by charge". The name is derived from the Japanese phrase O cha demo ikaga desuka, translating to English as "How about a cup of tea?", referring to the time it would take to charge a car.*

This type of charger looks like a typical petrol pump-sized machine. It can add 60 to 100 miles of range an electric car in just 20 minutes of charging.

Figure 56: Level 3 DC Fast Charger

Unfortunately, CHAdeMO charging infrastructure did not grow very fast. The reason being that other automakers lobbied against CHAdeMO deployment because it was not an SAE authorized standard. It was standard co-developed by TEPCO (Tokyo Electric Power Company) and the Japanese automakers. Instead of adopting CHAdeMO, the SAE developed their own fast charging standard (Combo Charging System), Tesla Motors developed a proprietary fast charging system (Supercharger), and the Chinese developed a different fast charging standard.

Emergence of CCS/SAE Combo type of DC fast Chargers

When SAE was asked to develop a DC fast charging system by non-Japanese automakers, the SAE J1772 committee basically took the existing J1772 plug and added on two large pins for high power DC. The upper part is the ordinary J1772 plug used in the USA, and the lower portion are the two DC power pins.

Among the reasons the J1772 committee developed CCS are single charging inlet to support slow and fast charging (versus two required for CHAdeMO)

Since the same connector serves multiple purposes, it allows car makers more freedom by needing only a single charging port in the skin of the car.

Also, going forward, smart grid protocols would be used to control charging. The point being the control protocol between the car and the charging station. CCS uses PLC for this communication, whereas CHAdeMO uses CAN. It must be noted that CAN is a data protocol used between components inside cars, whereas the PLC is part of the smart grid protocols. Therefore, the smart grid connectivity would be better served by CCS type of chargers.

As can be seen from the above picture, there are four or so DC Fast Charging systems currently being used by electric car manufacturers. The picture shows four different connectors.

At the current moment the leading car for each type is:

- CHAdeMO—Nissan Leaf
- CCS/SAE Combo—BMW i3
- China GB/T—Chinese Models

DC fast-charge stations generally support both standards. All carmakers adhere to one of these standards, except Tesla, which has developed a higher-performance charging station, "Super Charger" but offers a CHAdeMO adapter as an option.

"Tesla Super Charger"

Since Tesla considers itself to be the market maker in the EVs world, it took advantage of the fact that there is no single standard for fast-charging. Therefore, it developed what it calls Tesla Superchargers which have a max power output of 120 kW. These super-fast charging stations can charge a Tesla battery in about 20 minutes and are being widely installed across the United States.

	System A CHAdeMO (Japan)	System B GB/T (PRC)	System C COMBO1 (US)	COMBO2 (DE)
Connector		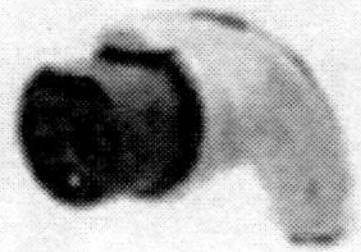		
Vehicle Inlet	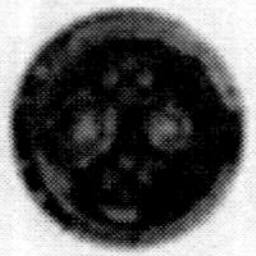	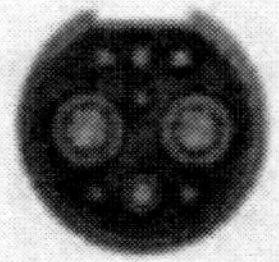		
Communication Protocol	CAN		PLC	

Figure 57: IEC DC Charging Systems

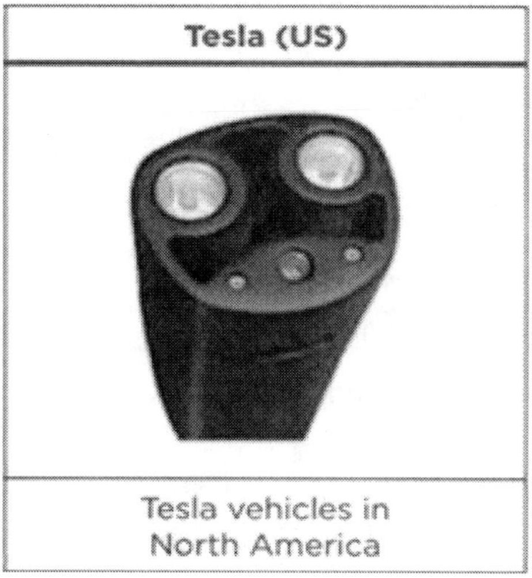

Figure 58: Tesla (US) Super Charger Port

It must be noted that:

- The Tesla mobile charging unit comes with adapters for every kind of power outlet, from 120 volt 12 amp (NEMA 5–20), through to 240 volt 50 amp (NEMA 14–50).
- Via an adapter, it can connect to J1772 charging stations.
- At a Supercharger station (pictured above) it can receive DC fast charging at up to a 120 kW rate.

It means a Tesla Model S or Model X owner can get rapid charging in a wide range of situations. Tesla Motors also sells an add-on adapter allowing a Model S/X owner to recharge at a CHAdeMO station.

Emergence of Induction Chargers

Another type of chargers based on inductive charging are coming into vogue. Inductive charging (also known as wireless charging or cordless charging) uses an electromagnetic field to transfer energy between two objects through electromagnetic induction.

Advantages of inductive (wireless) charging

It has several advantages such as:

- Ease of operation and amenable to automation of the charging process.
- User comfort as no cable connections are required and the driver can simply drive over the induction plate to charge. Great advantage in adverse weather conditions.
- Automated charging as the inductive charger is placed on the parking slot, at home or at work.
- The system is safe against vandalism, misuse/abuse and environmental influences (e.g. humidity) because all devices are encapsulated in the vehicle and the ground.
- There is no negative impact on the cityscape (all devices are hidden in the ground).

Figure 59: Induction Charging Station; Source: google

One innovative player called **PLUGLESS** is popularizing wireless inductive chargers for existing EVs also as shown in the Figure 59.

Over and above, the earlier mentioned stationary charging advantages being the inductive charging offers many more possibilities for en-route charging.

The potential of inductive en-route charging

With inductive en-route charging, EVs could be charged while standing at the traffic light, the bus stop or the taxi stand while it should be impracticable with the conductive charging option. So, using wireless inductive charging, these short timeframes could be used to charge the EV and hence its range. The charging method above is called static inductive en-route charging because the vehicle is standing still while charging.

In addition, there is also the possibility to charge the vehicle while it is actually moving. This charging method is called dynamic inductive en-route charging. This charging method holds the potential of giving the driver virtually limitless range as long as he stays on paths specifically adapted for dynamic inductive en-route charging.

Figure 60: Induction Charging based on DEVC technology

QUALCOMM is a leading proponent of this technology and it has developed what it calls Qualcomm Halo dynamic electric vehicle charging (DEVC). Based on the DEVC technology many new innovations in inductive charging are coming into vogue which allow cars to charge both while parked and while on the road.

Implications for India

Given this backdrop and the fact that the penetration of EVs is still minuscule in India, the choices are many. Some of the decisions making that need to be made are:

1. Adoption of a specific charger protocol given the scenario possibly for India, SAE combo would be a more appropriate choice.
2. India could also like in Telecom, leapfrog directly to wireless inductive technology. This has advantage as India has relatively less public space and propensity to vandalize public infrastructure is high. This technology would take care of both the above aspects. However, the costs factors could be huge in short run.
3. The other emerging competitors such as Battery Swapping may makes sense in a country like India, which has wholeheartedly adopted 'sharing economy'. The current bottleneck is non-standardization of batteries used in EVs.
4. In a still futuristic scenario, flow batteries or metal air batteries may become technology of choice whereby the existing fossil fuel infrastructure can be revamped to fill fresh electrolyte in such batteries and remove spent electrolyte.

CHAPTER SIX

DEVELOPING EV CHARGING INFRASTRUCTURE

Introduction

India has set an ambitious goal to leapfrog to electric mobility, pathway to this goal is establishing an appropriate and widespread charging infrastructure. It is well known that proper infrastructure is to key to success. British administrators created railway infrastructure in India about 170 years ago, and since then it has become life line of Indian economy. Therefore, for EVs to become mainstream, India must establish its EV charging infrastructure. Given the current predominance of Lithium-ion batteries, the creation of EV charging stations or "EVSE" is of paramount importance.

Figure 61: Solar enabled Charging Infrastructure

The growth in the propagation of electric vehicles (EVs) will only happen if appropriate charging infrastructure is available. But then it is like proverbial "*chicken-and-egg*" story as to what comes first. Commercially, entrepreneurs will not invest in charging infrastructure without a realistic assessment of the size of EVs market in the future. Ideally, both the vehicle market and the infrastructure should grow simultaneously. In this piece, we would primarily discuss the developments and significance of charging infrastructure across various geographies, how different types of business models for charging infrastructure will develop and the implications for India.

Typically, there are two ways to approach development of charging infrastructure. In the first approach which is utopian is to develop complete electric vehicle charging network in one go. Though, this could promote a rapid uptake of EVs, but return on such capital will not be viable. The other model is the build based on incremental growth which implies enlarging the infrastructure as user demands increase over time.

Naturally, it is second model that is more acceptable. Simultaneously, customers should also be incentivized in other ways such reducing the taxes, lower tariff of electricity being used charging EVs among others, to propagate rapid adoption.

Further, as technology is rapidly changing, varieties of models are emerging apart from usual conductive type. Even in conductive type, there are multiple kinds of chargers that are in vogue. These create additional imponderables for an investors.

Global Scenario

Today, the Global Electric Vehicle (EV) Charging Infrastructure industry is valued at 1.20Bn USD. It is expected to grow at a CAGR of 48% over the period 2017–2025.

As technological innovations are rapidly upgrading current EV

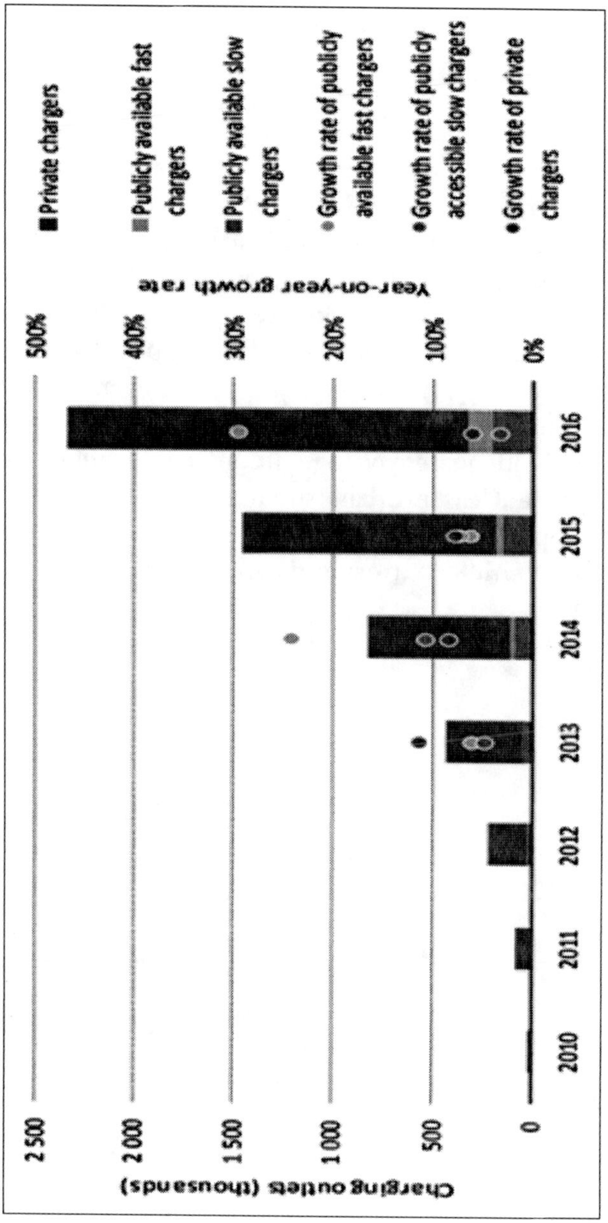

Figure 62: Penetration of Conductive type Charges till 2016

models and bringing them to near parity with current IC engine based cars. We can see further growth in charging infrastructure.

Europe

Europe has taken an approach of multiplayer participation in the development of charging infrastructure through a combination of private charge point providers (PPP), power companies, automakers, and governments. To rapidly enlarge charging infrastructure in order to create rapid transition to electric vehicle, they have also created several funding schemes and PPP models. At present in the European Union, there is a huge priority focus on EVs and their charging infrastructure. They have even issued the guidelines to ensure that recharging points accessible to the public are built up with adequate coverage, in order to enable electric vehicles to circulate at least in urban/suburban agglomerations and other densely populated areas. The focus is to install infrastructure that recharges vehicle batteries quickly, to accommodate longdistance trips.

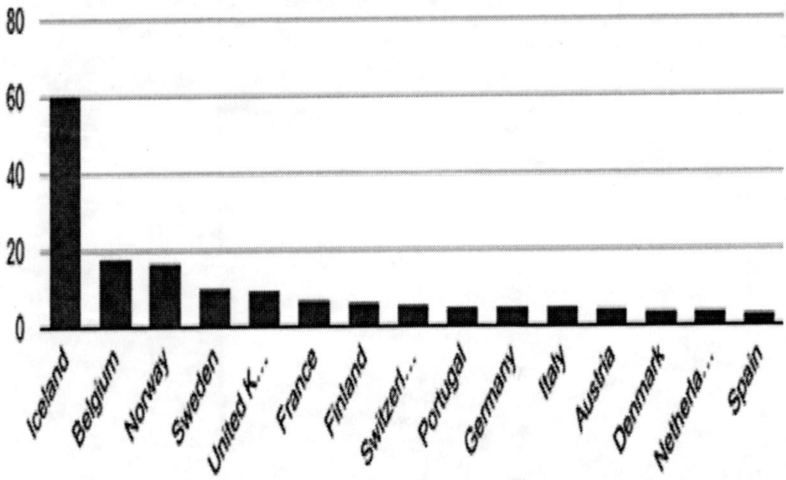

Figure 63: No. of PEV per Charging Position in European countries; Source: From the website of European Alternative Fuels Observatory

North America

In order to achieve mass acceptance and deployment of electric vehicles in North America, the two large countries have taken different approaches.

Canada has recognized that charging and maintenance infrastructure for EVs must become widely available throughout their nation. Creation of charging infrastructure in Canada has been primarily through a number of provincial and local governments funded public programs. In fact, the federal government is also actively involved in the sector.

A policy is being created for a zero-emission vehicle strategy which aims to set new goals for electrification and its associated charging infrastructure. To achieve this, a large funding support of CAD 182.5 million for electric vehicle charging and hydrogen fueling infrastructure has been committed.

The U.S. EV market continues to be bullish and is fast growing. Through the American Recovery and Reinvestment Act of 2009, (ARR) largely pushed federal funding through the EV project and it essentially created the charging infrastructure in the US.

As a result, in about six years, the number of charging points have grown to 36,000. Almost all of these government-funded stations are operated by private networks.

Asia

China is the definite leader, when it comes to adoption rate of EV and associated infrastructure in Asia. Similar to Europe, in China too, the charging infrastructure is multiplayer game which includes the central government, local governments, and utilities.

The fast development of charging network serves China's ambitions to become a major player in EV market globally in the years ahead. China aims to reach a figure of about 7 million EVs by 2025.

To complement this audacious goal, the charging infrastructure has expanded dramatically in China in the past few years. The cities are mandated to provide one charge point for every 8 electric vehicles, and charging stations should be no farther than 1 km from any point within the center area of the city.

Also, to promote EV sales, some automakers in China have constructed charging stations in specific regions to propagate easy use of EVs. Today, China represents almost half of the global supply of electric vehicle charging infrastructure.

Ever since the introduction of modern electric vehicles in **Japan** in 2011, the government and the country's major automakers have supported creation of charging infrastructure, viewing it as a key requirement for increasing electric vehicle sales. In 2013, the government created the massive **Next Generation Vehicle Charging Infrastructure Deployment Promotion Project** to fund charging stations around cities and highway rest stations.

The Development Bank of Japan partnering with leading Japanese car makers and power company TEPCO, created an entity the Nippon Charge Service (NCS), which created a nationwide network of charging stations now operated as a private joint venture leading development of almost 7,500 stations.

Various Types of EV Charging Infrastructure

Different kinds of charging infrastructure are emerging to support the various technological developments of EVs. However, currently Lithium-ion batteries dominate the battery space for EVs, therefore largely infrastructure plays focused on conductive type of charging, i.e., **with a wired plug.**

		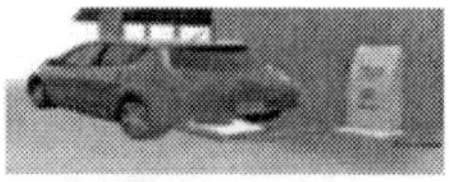
Wired charging using a plug	Battery swapping	Induction charging
Plugging in to a charging station using a cable and plug	Replacing a battery for a fully charged one at swapping station	Battery in the car is charged by wireless induction charging
4-8 hrs (Slow) 20-30 min (Fast)	5 min	2-8 hrs[2]
PHEV, BEV, EREV	Special BEV	Special BEV

Figure 64: Three types of Charging Infrastructure currently supports vehicles powered by LIBs

Conductive Wired Charging using a plug

The conductive type charging infrastructure is currently classified into three categories based on speed: Level 1, Level 2, and Level 3 (DC) fast charging.

Charging connector standards used for charging electric vehicles may vary from place to place. Although, the most common plug types are generally well-defined and each works well for its specific application, the variety of standards has led to lack of uniformity by the industry and thus inconveniencing the users.

The Table below from SAE summarizes current state of various EV chargers currently in vogue, it includes both AC and DC chargers. It proposes the development of AC Type 3 and DC Type 2 & 3 Chargers in the future.

AC level 1 (SAE J1772™)	PEV includes on-board charger	*DC Level 1	EVSE includes an off-board charger
	120V, 1.4 kW @ 12 amp 120V, 1.9 kW @ 16 amp		200-450 V DC, up to 36 kW (80 A)
	Est. charge time:		Est. charge time (20 kW off-board charger):
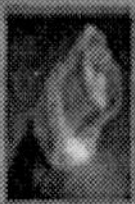	PHEV: 7hrs (SOC* - 0% to full)		PHEV: 22 min. (SOC* - 0% to 80%)
	BEV: 17hrs (SOC – 20% to full)		BEV: 1.2 hrs. (SOC – 20% to 100%)
AC level 2 (SAE J1772™)	PEV includes on-board charger (see below for different types)	*DC Level 2	EVSE includes an off-board charger
	240 V, up to 19.2 kW (80 A)		200-450 V DC, up to 90 kW (200 A)
	Est. charge time for 3.3 kW on-board charger		Est. charge time (45 kW off-board charger):
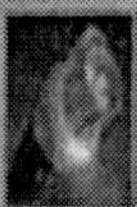	PEV: 3 hrs (SOC* - 0% to full)		PHEV: 10 min. (SOC* - 0% to 80%)
	BEV: 7 hrs (SOC – 20% to full)		BEV: 20 min. (SOC – 20% to 80%)
	Est. charge time for 7 kW on-board charger		
	PEV: 1.5 hrs (SOC* - 0% to full)	*DC Level 3 (TBD)	EVSE includes an off-board charger
	BEV: 3.5 hrs (SOC – 20% to full)		200-600V DC (proposed) up to 240 kW (400 A
	Est. charge time for 20 kW on-board charger		Est. charge time (45 kW off-board charger):
	PEV: 22 min. (SOC* - 0% to full)		BEV (only): <10 min. (SOC* - 0% to 80%)
	BEV: 1.2 hrs (SOC – 20% to full)		
*AC Level 3 (TBD)	> 20 kW, single phase and 3 phase		

*Not finalized
Voltages are nominal configuration voltages, not coupler ratings
Rated Power is at nominal configuration operating voltage and coupler rated current
Ideal charge times assume 90% efficient chargers, 150W to 12V loads and no balancing of Traction Battery Pack

Notes:
1) BEV (25 kWh usable pack size) charging always starts at 20% SOC, faster than a 1C rate (total capacity charged in one hour) will also stop at 80% SOC instead of 100%
2) PHEV can start from 0% SOC since the hybrid mode is available.

Developed by the SAE Hybrid Committee ver. 031

Figure 65: SAE Charging Configuration and Rating Terminology

Battery Swapping Stations (BSS)

The other type of charging infrastructure that is slowly emerging is based on the premise of battery swapping. However, again the issue of non-standardization of battery stymie this approach.

Figure 66: Battery Swapping

Despite the fact that the number of battery charging locations is increasing, however the charging time at these stations is either too long or reduce battery life by forcing them to undergo fast charging processes. As an alternative to these charging stations recently there has been emergence of Battery Swapping Stations (BSS). As name suggests, they swap a customer's discharged battery with a fully charged one of the same type.

This also create an interesting business model, there is a thought that adoption of EVs is limited due to the high cost of the batteries. This model separates the ownership of batteries from that of the vehicle. In this scenario, batteries are owned by third party who is also responsible for swapping them at an appropriate juncture. This reduces the cost of ownership of the EVs. Standardized batteries can be swapped out with fully charged batteries after they are drained. A network of swapping stations, similar to petrol pumps, will facilitate the swapping of batteries. Payment models include leasing the batteries and pay-per-use.

BSS acts as a battery aggregator and has enough clout to participate in markets for electrical energy and reserve. The BSS can maximize its profits by providing services to the system, such as voltage support, regulation reserves, or energy arbitrage. This is shown in the Figure 67.

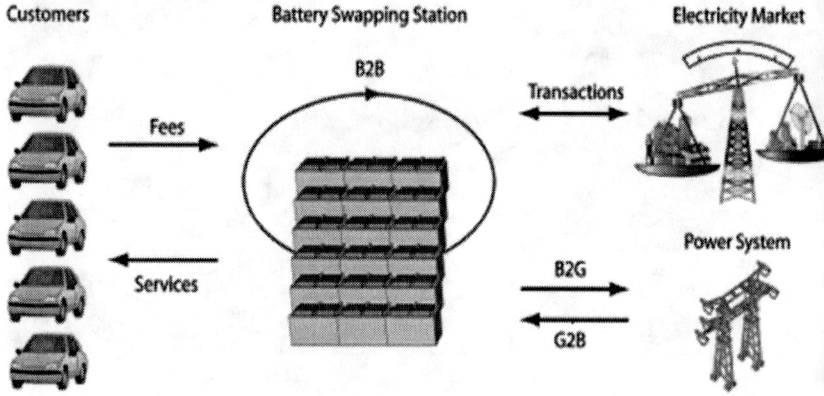

Figure 67: Battery Swapping – interactions with customers, market & power system

However, battery swapping model has not fully succeeded globally due to techno-commercial dynamics. As is known, the main issues are around standardization, commercial viability and reliability.

On face of it, it seems that, in India the entire premise of 'battery swapping' with leasing/pay-per-use model may significantly lower the acquisition cost of the EV. Perhaps, swapping proves to be of great advantage for fleet operators, low speed EVs (e.g., taxi aggregators, e-auto, e-rickshaw etc) and busses with intercity point to point travel (< 30 km per trip, 8–10 trips per day). A well-established network of smart swappable batteries could be instrumental in rapid adoption of EVs for public transportation. However, the **roadblocks still remain** which are:

- **Standardization of EV Lithium Ion Battery Packs** has not happened globally. The probability of this happening in

India is questionable. This is so because, majority of the auto OEMs preferring to control their design strategies for battery packs as their core technology.

- **Commercially Viable Business Models,** since Indian government is eschewing subsidies to create a viable non-subsidized commercially sound model is extremely important.
- **Reliability of Leased/Rented Battery Packs** gets accentuated in India. In quest of achieving profitability, if battery providers short change the customer and therefore causing a potential breach may lead to a serious disaster of swapping business and can create larger controversies as well.

Induction Charging Infrastructure

Inductive charging (also known as wireless charging or cordless charging) uses an electromagnetic field to transfer energy between two objects through electromagnetic induction. This is usually done with a charging station.

This offers several advantages over the conductive (using a cable) charging method:

- Ease of operation and amenable to automation of the charging process.
- User comfort as no cable connections are required and the driver can simply drive over the induction plate to charge. Great advantage in adverse weather conditions.
- Automated charging as the inductive charger is placed on the parking slot, at home or at work.
- The system is safe against vandalism, misuse/abuse and environmental influences (e.g. humidity) because all devices are encapsulated in the vehicle and the ground.
- There is no negative impact on the city-scape (all devices are hidden in the ground).

These above mentioned advantages already prove the usefulness of (stationary) inductive charging compared to the currently more common conductive charging infrastructure. Inductive charging offers many more possibilities especially concerning en-route charging.

Figure 68: Inductive en-route Charging at a Parking Area

With inductive en-route charging, EVs could be charged while standing at the traffic light, the bus stop or the taxi stand while it should be impracticable with the conductive charging option. So, using wireless inductive charging, these short time-frames could be used to charge the EV and hence its range. The charging method above is called static inductive en-route charging because the vehicle is standing still while charging.

In addition, there is also the possibility to charge the vehicle while it is actually moving. This charging method is called dynamic inductive en-route charging. This charging method holds the potential of giving the driver virtually limitless range as long as he stays on paths specifically adapted for dynamic inductive en-route charging.

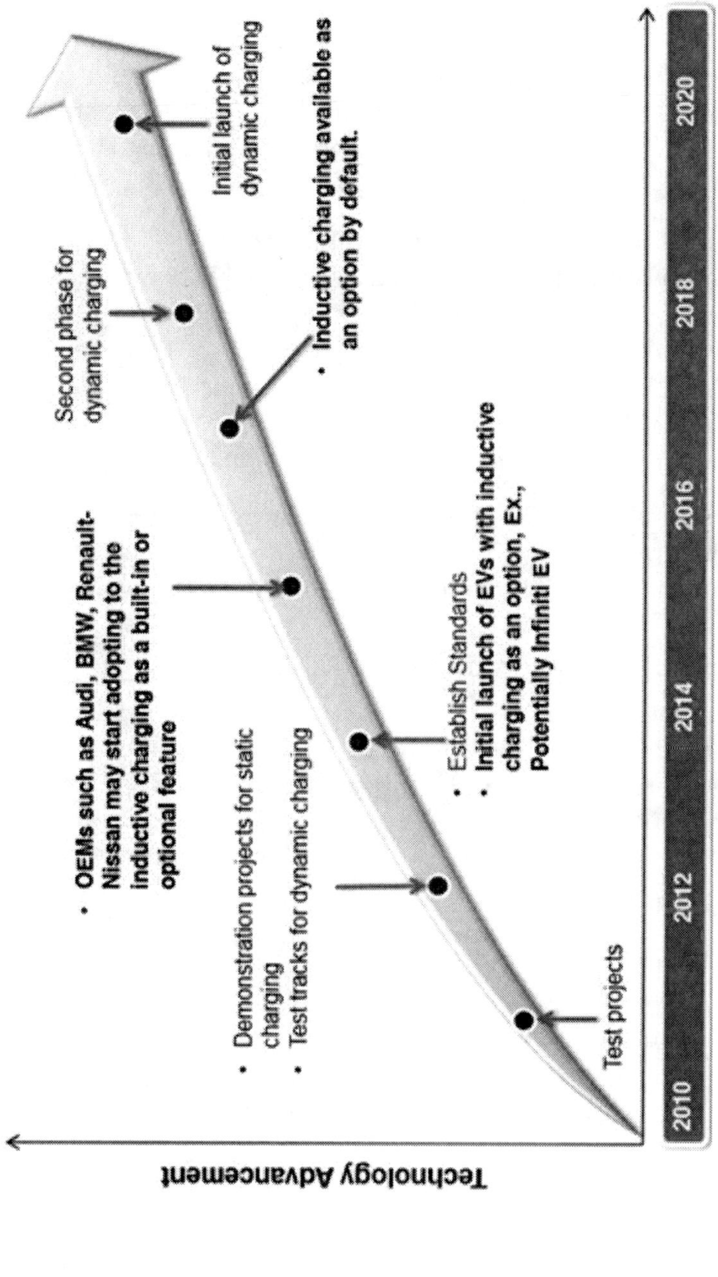

Figure 69: Inductive Charging for EVs, Future Market Trends

Flow Battery Infrastructure

Recent research excitement to make flow batteries commercially viable is driven by issues around charging infrastructure of current LIBs. Such batteries have technical advantages over conventional rechargeable ones.

In flow batteries, separate liquid tanks (for anolyte and catholyte) can be mounted on the car itself (just like current gasoline tanks) and thereby unlimited longevity can be achieved. Electrolyte stored in this manner is usually pumped through the cells of the battery. They can be rapidly "recharged" by replacing the electrolyte liquid (in a similar way to refilling fuel tanks of IC engines) while simultaneously recovering the spent material for re-energization.

Once this technology becomes commercialized, the charging stations for them would be very similar to current gasoline filling stations. An artist's conception of such station is shown as below.

Implications for India

Given this backdrop and the fact that the penetration of EVs is still minuscule in India, it is important that as a country we make decisions regarding charging infrastructure which would be useful in long run:

1. In case of conductive charging, adoption of a specific charger protocol would be essential. We think SAE combo charger would be a more appropriate choice.
2. We could also just like we did in case of Telecom, leapfrog directly to wireless inductive technology. This has many advantages such as, India has relatively less public space, and our propensity to vandalize public infrastructure is high. This technology would take care of both the above aspects. However, the costs factors could be huge in short run, but in long run it would justify.
3. Though, the concept of Battery Swapping makes imminent sense in a country like India, which has wholeheartedly

adopted 'sharing economy'. The current bottleneck as we mentioned is non-standardization of batteries and in absence of subsidies a commercial viable model.

4. In a still futuristic scenario, flow batteries or metal air batteries may become technology of choice whereby the existing fossil fuel infrastructure can be revamped to fill fresh electrolyte in such batteries and remove spent electrolyte.

CHAPTER SEVEN

MAJOR CHALLENGES FOR EV POLICY

After setting an audacious goal of having 100% electric mobility by 2030, as announced by India's Minister of Transportation in September 2017, we now find a situation of electrifying confusion on the same. At the government level, different people make contradicting statements and as always is the case in this country, that clear policy does not emerge.

Obviously, the lack of unified thinking among the government circle is quite visible when the Transport Minister says in January 2018 that the EV Policy has been drafted by NITI Aayog and was awaiting for the cabinet approval. Then, he backtracks from this statement, a month later, saying that as such there was no need for EV policy. As a rejoinder, Vice Chairman of NITI Aayog suggests that India needs an EV policy, though the priority should be onto two-wheeler and public transportation. We, as a nation, should focus on how to get this huge segment of electric mobility and not focus on cars.

There is more to this issue than meets the eye. In fact, the underlying issues for such backtracking and confusion seems to be because of the triple spectre which haunts India's electric mobility odyssey. Let us briefly look into these three factors.

1. Reality of abatement of Carbon Footprint

Electric vehicles reduce pollution only if a high percentage of the electricity mix comes from renewable sources and if the battery manufacturing takes place at a site far from the vehicle use region. Industries developed due to increased electric vehicle adoption may also cause additional air pollution.

One of the primary aspects of the audacious goal set for electric mobility was to deliver multiple co-benefits implying improved environment, energy security and renewable integration. Therefore, there was an imperative that there would be a domestic EV policy to improve competitiveness of electric vehicles.

According to a Niti Aayog-Rocky Mountain Institute (RMI) report, India can save 64% of anticipated passenger road-based mobility-related energy demand and 37% of carbon emissions in 2030 by pursuing a shared, electric, and connected mobility future.

A paper published by some IIM Ahmedabad researchers builds various scenarios of EVs penetration. In a "business-as-usual" scenario, the overall transportation energy requirements increases nearly six fold between 2010 and 2015. The overall dependence on fossil fuels continues despite some diversification towards natural gas and bio-fuels. However, after 2020, electricity starts emerging as significant option, based on transportation for intercity passengers, freight movements, implementation of metro projects and diffusion of EVs (buses, cars, two/three wheelers). As per this model, the share of EVs in overall electricity demand rises from about 54% in 2020 to 67% in 2050.

In case of aggressive penetration of EV scenario, the overall demand of energy is lower because of the fact that EVs are more energy efficient. However, with addition of Low Carbon Society (LCS is attached to a global stabilization target of 2°C.) coupled with EVs scenario, the energy demand further reduces. These are presented in the Figures 71 & 72.

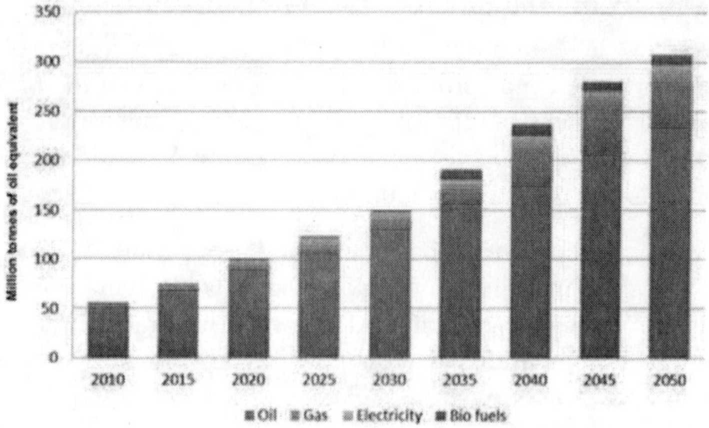

Figure 70: Fuel Mix for Transport in BAU scenario

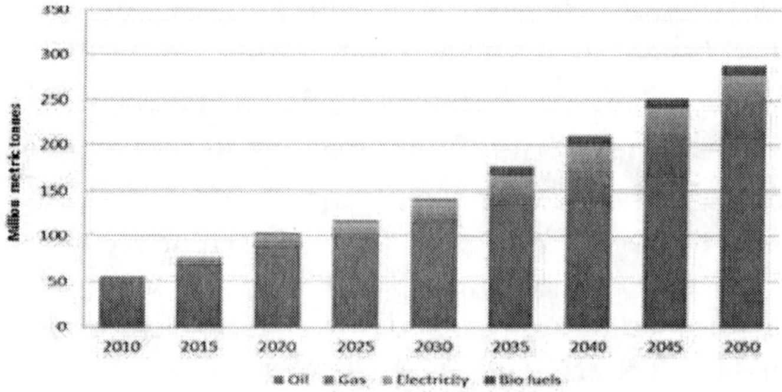

Figure 71: Fuel mix transport in EV

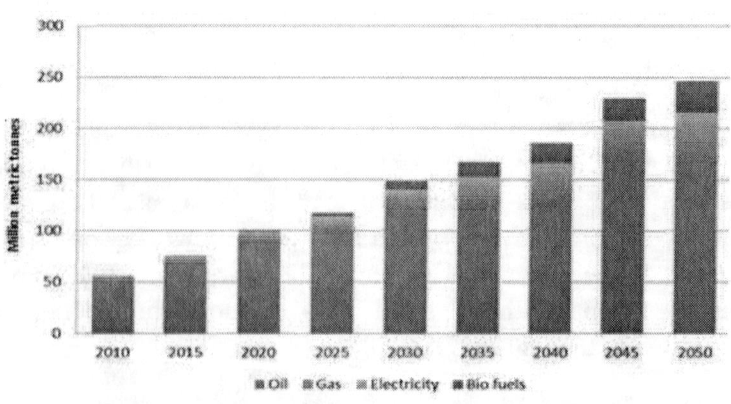

Figure 72: Fuel Mix for transport in EV-LCS scenario

It also means that if we have to achieve LCS goals, it is imperative that India's EV policy document (as and when developed) must mandate use of renewable energy resources for charging of electric vehicles. This would also help Indian renewable energy generation companies who are developing about 175 GW capacity including 100 GW from solar by 2022. Essentially, the fates of solar power and EVs in India are intertwined, provided that EVs have batteries that can offer a storage solution to India's clean energy push.

Solar power generated during the day needs to be stored in batteries. The storage capability of EV batteries could help with grid balancing. This may mitigate a perceived risk that EV charging would lead to intermittent surge in electricity demand. This may lead to break down of India's already stretched electricity distribution networks.

As seen in all the three cases presented earlier that EVs would lead to fresh demand for electricity – the lack of which is weighing down the entire power sector. Any uptake in demand for power will help improve the financial viability of currently stressed power sector projects.

Therefore, government is under dilemma whether to have a policy document that mandates only use of renewable energy for EV charging or to have those currently stressed power assets also have a play. Certainly, it is a tough decision to make. If the currently stressed power stations (which are largely fossil fuel based) get a play, then the role of reduction of carbon footprint would not be achieved for a country that still needs 75% of its electricity needs through fossil fuels. Some may argue that the introduction of EVs would simply move the pollution of city roads to its hinder lands where power is generated.

2. Impact on India's Auto-components Industry

The Indian auto-components industry has experienced healthy growth over the last few years. It has grown to reach a level of Rs

2.92 lakh crore (US$ 43.52 billion) in FY 2016-17 and is further expected to grow by 8-10 % in FY 2017-18. As per an estimate by the Automotive Component Manufacturers Association of India (ACMA), the Indian auto-components industry is likely to reach a turnover of US$ 100 billion by 2020 backed by strong exports.

The auto-component industry accounts for almost 7 % of India's GDP and employs as many as 25 million people, both directly and indirectly. A stable government framework, increased purchasing power, large domestic market, and an ever increasing development in infrastructure have made this possible.

Currently, the auto-component industry is deeply worried about the rapid transformation of the industry, from internal combustion engines (ICE) to EVs. In this regard, ACMA the industry lobby represented their deep concern to NITI Aayog in December last year. The key points they lobbied were the industry investments and the massive job losses and the country cannot afford to lose the domestic component industry in its rapid propagation drive for EVs.

It is indeed a sincere appeal, given the fact that internal combustion engines, which are used in most cars, have more than 2,000 moving parts, while an electric vehicle has about 20, resulting in fewer breakdowns. Among the parts that will dry up demand once EVs dominate in India are the engines, transmission, aluminum castings, cylinder blocks and cast iron. The graphic below shows that taken together these constitute almost 50% of the industry. Such components will be replaced by electric motor which will run by batteries.

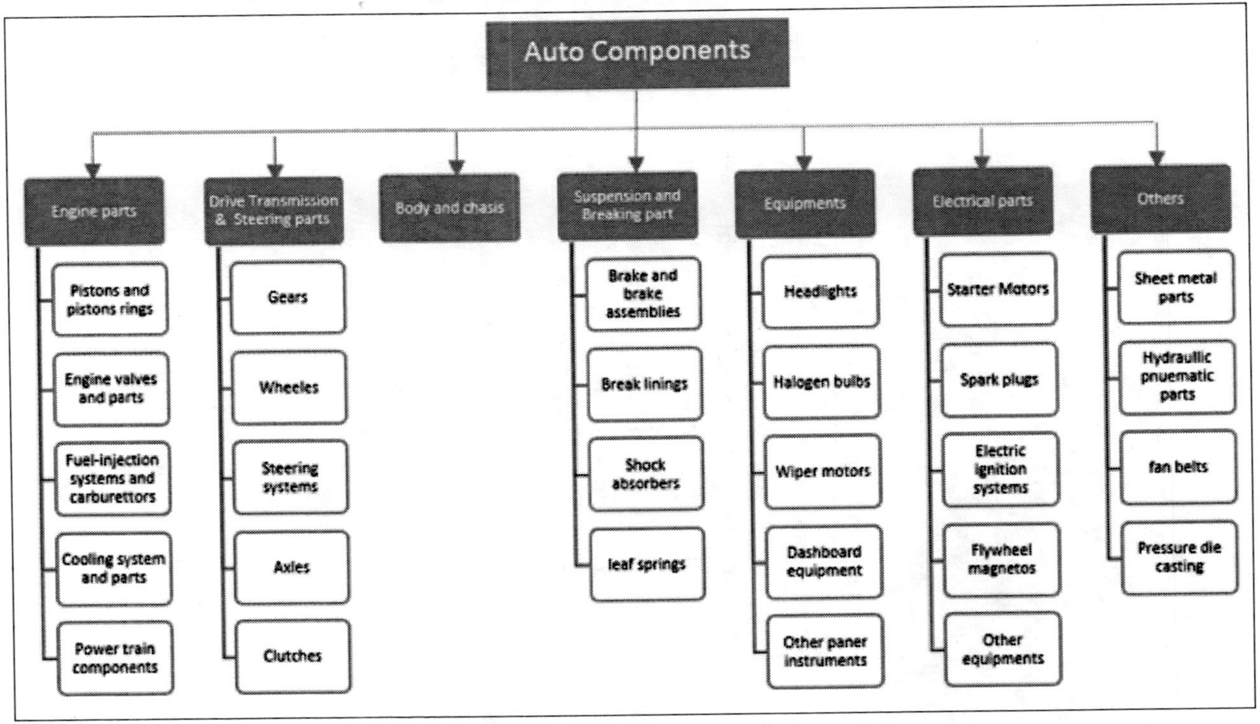

Figure 73: Structure of Indian Auto-Component Industry;
Source: Automotive Component Manufacturers Association of India

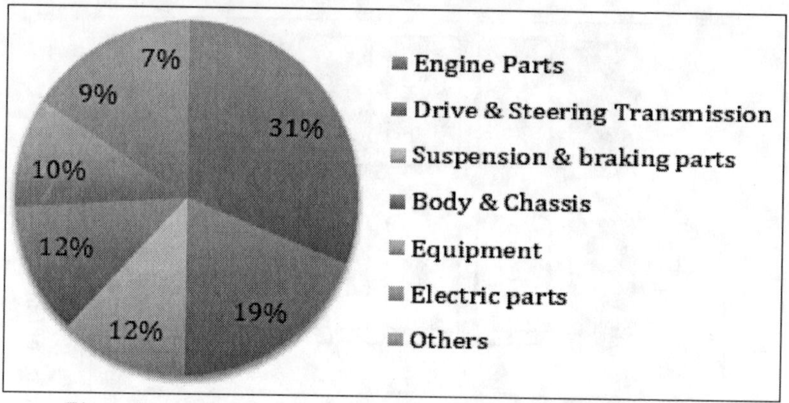

Figure 74: Sectoral break-up of Auto-component Industry in India

Also, the another anxiety expressed by the ACMA is that the ICE powertrain contributes to over 60% of the employment generation in the auto component sector, and that a switch to 100% electric could impact up to 5.6 million jobs by 2025-26.

Following the global trend, the Indian auto-components industry is expected to follow OEMs in adoption of electric vehicle technologies. The global move towards electric vehicles will generate new opportunities for automotive suppliers. The mass conversion to electric vehicles may generate a US$ 300 billion domestic market for EV batteries in India by 2030.

The emergence of electric vehicles means a new ecosystem will have to be built and a lot of component manufacturers will have to adapt and transform to make the appropriate components and sub-assemblies for EVs.

However, another fear is that for adoption of technology for EVs our industry is 7-8 years behind global peers, which can significantly erode competitive advantage of our local component industry.

Given the fact that this industry contributes substantially to GDP and job growth, it is very preeminently is the poster boy of Indian manufacturing story. On one hand, the government is propagating various initiatives such as Make in India and is very keen in improving the employability opportunities of India's young population. On the other hand, it wants rapid proliferation of EVs to meet the global targets of carbon footprint mitigation. SIAM (Society for Indian Automobile Manufactures) has, in concurrence with the NITI Aayog come up with a via-media that 40% of vehicles in India would be shifted to electric while vehicles used for public transport would be 100% shifted to electric by 2030.

This is another behind the scene issue that faces government in coming out with a definitive policy on EVs. They are likely wait till checks and balances between two opposing key initiatives are thought through.

3. Threat of Electronic Components Import Bill exceeding the Petroleum Import Bill

A major thought process behind India's ambitious target of 100% electric mobility is to drastically reduce the crude oil import bill. According to a Niti Aayog-Rocky Mountain Institute (RMI) report, adoption of EVs would result in a reduction of 156 Mtoe in diesel and petrol consumption by 2030. At $52/bbl of crude, this would imply a net savings of roughly Rs 3.9 lakh crore (approximately $60 billion) in that year.

The writing is on the wall – as a technology, battery costs will continue to decline as manufacturing and the chemistry improves. Oil companies can reduce costs, but commodities don't see costs decline in the same way. Finite natural resources see costs rise as they become scarcer. The possibility that oil remains cheap indefinitely would only be because EVs destroy demand. As per a Bloomberg estimate, the EVs could capture 35 percent of the market by 2040, which would displace 13 mb/d.

All this is fine in principle, but the following data shows a very disturbing trend for India.

As we see from the above graph, petroleum product constitute

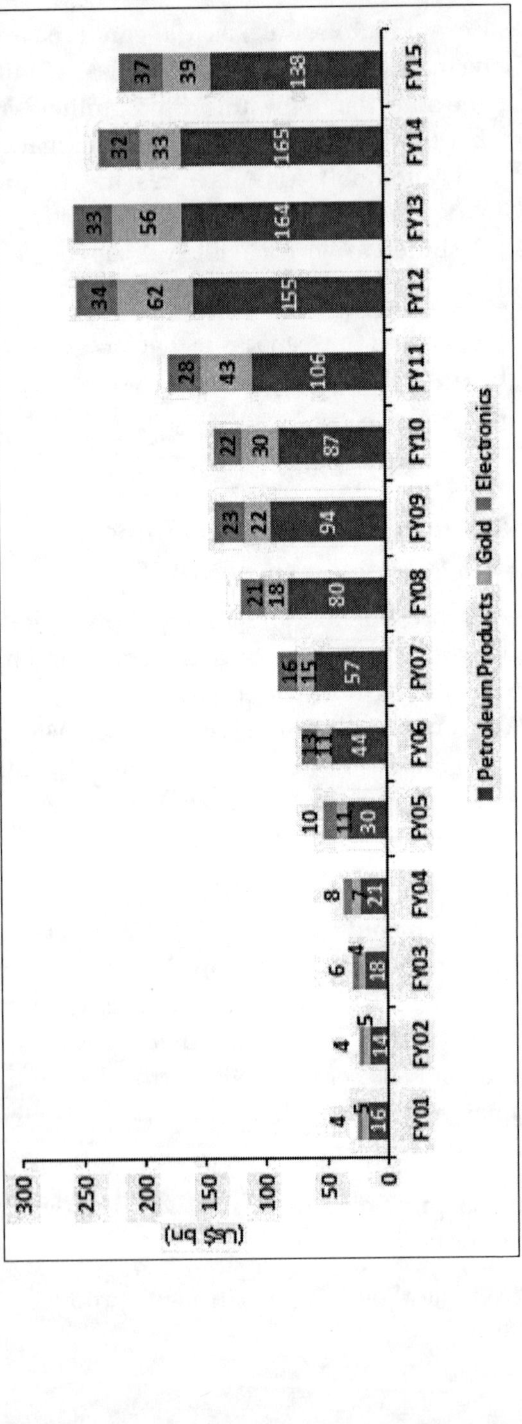

Figure 75: India's Import Bill on Petroleum Products, Gold & Electronics 2001-2015

by far the largest segment of India's import bill. However, this is going to change soon as electronic good will surpass the oil bill by 2020.

This is because India is one of the largest growing electronics markets in the world with an estimated size of US$69.6 billion in 2012. With a CAGR of 24%, it is expected to surpass the US$400 billion mark by 2020. However, sharp growth in demand for electronic goods is unlikely to translate to higher domestic production, which is currently at US$32.7 billion and likely to cross US$104 billion by 2022. While the domestic industry will cater to only a fourth of this demand, India will still need to import goods worth US$300 billion, roughly equivalent to the country's oil import bill. Till 2015, electronics imports at US$37 billion were the third highest import item next only to crude and gold.

Now, India is staring at an import nightmare of an unprecedented rise in proportion of electronic goods that can push the country into a spiral of high imports. This would necessarily entail higher external and internal borrowings and does not bode well for India's economy in the long term.

India's electronic goods production was inadequate to meet demand due to deficiency in skill level to compete with imported products. Hence, to meet the rising demand, India is heavily dependent on import of electronics goods from China, US and other South East Asian regions. If we dig deep, the main reason behind the rising import of electronic goods is shortfall in domestic production. Local production faces a substantial cost disadvantage constraining investment in plants and equipment, technology absorption, development capability and innovation.

There is a possibility of double whammy surrounding India's EV programme, This is because India does not have enough lithium reserves for manufacturing lithium-ion batteries. This could lead to a substantial change in the country's energy security priorities, with securing lithium supplies, a key raw material for EV batteries, becoming as important as buying oil and gas fields overseas. So, on one hand the gains in reduction of oil import bill may get supplanted by securing lithium supply. On the other hand, in immediate run, the lithium batteries would again be imported from China and South Asian countries, leading to further bloating of India's electronic good import bill.

Indian auto ancillary firms are worried about the EV story going the solar module way with most solar power developers sourcing modules and equipment from countries such as China, where they are cheaper.

The lack of battery manufacturing in India is a real problem. If India is not able to get its act together quickly enough to get into the manufacturing of all these new sunrise industries associated with EV ecosystem. Even on batteries, the same thing is going to happen. Already, China is making massive investments at massive scales, and we are still thinking about it.

The delay in the EV policy is also possibility due to the fact to first get Electronics manufacturing policy in place to access from global networks of innovations and productions. This may result in indigenization of subassemblies and key components for EVs. Over the years, local manufacturers faced barriers in the form of restrictive regulations and a largely poor implementation of past policies, which stymied investments in plants and equipment, technology absorption and innovations. This could be attributed to high cost of finance at ~11-13% (cost of fund) against 2-4% globally, high power cost due to irregular power supply, etc. This, coupled with higher tax imposed by the Indian government, makes manufacturing of electronic products unviable in the country. All this has to change to make sure that the EV components (batteries, electric motors, electronic control modules) are made in India which will provide not only an alternative to auto ancillary industry, but also help in containing the electronic imports.

CHAPTER EIGHT

GLOBAL EV SCENARIO

Initiatives for Promoting Electric Vehicles

United States of America, France, United Kingdom, China, Norway, Japan and Netherlands are the global frontrunners in EV adoption. Some of the key policy measures and incentives in these countries are summarized below.

1. United States

The United States has enacted numerous national and incentive programs to expedite EV adoption. The Department of Energy had released the "EV Everywhere" initiative which focused on R&D and consumer awareness to achieve cost and market parity for EVs till 2022. Different states in the US have announced their individual EV policy frameworks, of which California has been the most successful.

Some of the support actions for EVs in California include:

- EV purchased during or after 2010 is eligible for a federal income tax credit of up to US$ 7,500
- Up to 2,500 USD income state tax credit rebate
- Special parking allowance
- Separate EV Charging Tariff
- Special access to high-occupancy vehicle lanes

- Public charging infrastructure and state private charging infrastructure
- Workplace charging infrastructure
- Low-carbon fuel norms and regulations
- State EV manufacturing initiatives
- Municipal and police EV fleets
- State transport EV fleet programs
- Shared e-mobility initiatives
- Target to convert 100% municipal fleet to run on alternative fuels by 2022

Many other states in the USA offer cash and non-cash incentives, such as carpool lane access and free parking. Some examples are:

- Arizona: Reduced vehicle license tax, carpool lane access and reduced electricity rates for EV charging
- Colorado: US$ 5,000 tax credit
- Hawaii: Carpool lane access and reduced electricity rates for EV charging
- Nevada: Carpool lane access and reduced electricity rates for EV charging
- New Jersey: Sales tax exemption
- Washington DC: Excise duty exemption

2. *France*

- Bonus-malus system: up to 6,300 euros grant for purchasing electric vehicles
- Incentive for diesel car scrap page: up to 3,700 euros
- 25% purchase subsidy on low-emission vehicles, e-mopeds or e-bikes
- 15% subsidy for diesel/gasoline vehicle replacement with EV
- Zero-cost parking

- Weekday ban on vehicles causing high pollution
- Tax incentives for charging station installation
- Grants and loans for private charging infrastructure installation
- Ongoing research and trials on EVs in public transport sector
- Target of converting entire bus fleet in Greater Paris to clean buses
- Introduction of electric delivery vans
- Shared e-mobility programs
- Fleet electrification targets for public transport fleets and private transport fleets like rentals and taxis

3. *United Kingdom*

- EVs (with CO_2 emissions below 100g/km) are exempt from the annual circulation tax, while other alternative fuel cars receive a GBP 10 discount on the paid rates.
- Pure electric cars are exempt from the company car tax, while all cars with CO_2 emissions lower than 50g/km pay 5% for the tax year 2015/2016
- EVs are exempted from congestion charges
- Plan to establish Central Ultra Low Emission Zone
- Electrification of public bus fleets
- Grants for home chargers
- Plan to build rapid EV charging infrastructure network along United Kingdom's Strategic Road Network

4. *China*

China has the largest global EV stock. The country has announced and implemented number of central and state level policies and strategies to encourage EV uptake.

- The electric utility State Grid Corporation has been involved in the construction of fast charging stations across the country. The country has laid down an aim of constructing at least one charging station per every two thousand EVs. It also aims to establish charging facilities sufficient to cater to the requirements of 5 million EVs by 2020.

- The "Ten Cities, Thousand Vehicles" program has grown to have a total of 25 cities. These pilot cities employed incentives, charging infrastructure, and other promotion activities to facilitate EV adoption. Many major cities have placed various restrictions on vehicle registrations to combat congestion and emission, for which relaxation has been provide to EVs.
- Shanghai city holds the record for greatest EV adoption in the country. It ranks as the leading city globally in terms of EV sales. The EV revolution has been given impetus in Shanghai as it was conferred the status of "International EV Demonstration City" by the Chinese Government. The city has a designated "EV Demonstration Zone" that is part of the Jiading District. The zone acts as a platform for congregation and communication between the EV stakeholders. The city EV goals have been supported with a number of central and regional level subsidies and tax exemptions on EV purchase. The city government has established numerous public charging stations and has also planned to deploy fast charging stations in the near future. Subsidy has been made available to businesses that aspire to enter the EV charging scene. Shared e-mobility has been encouraged through programs like "EVCARD" and also through the electrification of public bus fleets.
- Shenzhen has organized a variety of local schemes for EV adoption and establishment of charging infrastructure. Close to 500 million yuan (US$ 80 million) was spent by the Shenzhen government per year from 2009 to 2015 for subsidization of EV cars. The city has further committed to invest 5 billion yuan on charging facilities, EV purchase

subsidies, and EV adoption policies, in 2015. The electric buses in Shenzhen have been fully electrified since December 2017. There are presently, 16359 electric buses in Shenzhen. Apart from the fiscal incentives, Shenzhen has also provided other incentives such as preferential parking spaces and registration relaxations for encouraging EV uptake. The city is one of the pioneers in the world for electrification of bus fleets. BYD, one of the leading lithium ion battery and EV manufacturers, is headquartered in Shenzhen.

- Battery electric vehicles dominate the EV market in Beijing due to EV purchase subsidy that is not applicable to plug-in hybrid vehicle models. Beijing has placed restrictions on new vehicle registrations to reduce congestion and traffic in the city. EVs have been exempted from these restrictions. The city has launched various consumer awareness campaigns, prominent of which is "Electric Vehicle into Community". Beijing has established a "New Energy Vehicle Experience Centre" which informs the public regarding new energy vehicles and permits test drives in BAIC electric vehicles. The city also has "Beijing New Energy Vehicle Promotion Centre" and "Beijing Auto Museum" which hold EV test drive programs to raise awareness. Private and public car fleet electrification initiatives have also been implemented by the Beijing city government.

5. *Norway*

Norway is a pioneer of the EV revolution, in its efforts to reduce GHG emissions. The country generates most of its electricity through its hydropower plants. Norway has planned to harness this electricity to drive EV deployment and charging. Norway has set a 2020 target of reaching a CO_2 emission rate below 85 gm/km. This is applicable to the new passenger vehicles that will be launched. In order to facilitate these targets, Norway provided a number of progressive incentives for EV deployment that includes tax and toll exemptions, preferential parking benefits and the facility of free charging at certain EVSE stations. The government has also invested large funds for enabling charging infrastructure on highways.

- The city of Oslo is the global leader in terms of electric vehicle market penetration. Oslo has set defined targets EV to reduce GHG emissions by 40% from transportation sector in its Climate Budget. The city has also implemented various passenger traffic restrictions in order to curb GHG emissions along with its EV initiative.
- For promoting EV deployment the Oslo government has granted a number of fiscal incentives that include relaxation on import duties and purchase tax on EVs, and lowering or complete removal of taxes on toll and leasing. The city has also defined strict "low-emission zones", provided free parking for EVs at municipal parking spaces, implemented subsidized EV charging tariffs and granted "special lane access" for e-buses.
- Oslo has also invested heavily in public and private charging infrastructure installation and EV research, through collaborations with private sector companies and various research organizations.

Norway had previously implemented a mix of initiatives to promote e-mobility:

- Lower tax: EVs are subject to reduced circulation or road tax, and are exempt from VAT and other charges like registration fees. Moreover, tax on company EV cars is 50 percent lower than for traditional cars. Annual motor vehicle tax/road tax is lower too
- Free parking: Municipality-owned parking lots offer free parking for EVs
- Free or discounted road tolls and ferry costs: EV owners can use most toll roads and ferry connections for free. They

may have to pay a fee in the future, but rates could still be discounted

- Special transport lanes: EVs enjoy access to dedicated, fast-moving lanes for public transport
- Free battery-charging points: An increasing number of publicly-funded charging stations allow EV users to charge their cars for free.

6. *Japan*

- In 2013, Next Generation Vehicle Charging Infrastructure Deployment Promotion Project was launched to fund charging stations around cities and highway rest stations in 2013 and 2014
- CHAdeMO association was formed by the Tokyo Electric Power Company (TEPCO), Nissan, Mitsubishi and Fuji Heavy Industries (the manufacturer of Subaru vehicles) that developed the CHAdeMO fast charging system
- The Development Bank of Japan collaborated with a number of vehicle manufacturers and the power utility TEPCO to develop the Nippon Charge Service (NCS), a charging stations network spanning the country that is currently operated as a private joint venture
- The Japanese government has exempted new next generation vehicles from acquisition tax and tonnage tax
- Reduced tax rates on EV purchase
- Purchase subsidies for EVs
- Substantial investments in charging infrastructure. As of 2016, there were an estimated 40,000 EV charging stations in Japan and only about 34,000 gas stations
- The government has also set an ambitious goal of making all Japanese vehicles sold around the world at least partly powered by electricity by 2050.

7. Netherlands

- Netherlands has set a national target of 75,000 privately owned EVs by 2020, and 50% of all new cars sales plug-in electric—with minimum 30% of these vehicles fully electric—by 2025
- First action plan for EV adoption was published in 2009 with an investment of nearly 65 million euros
- Establishment of the Formula E-Team, a national public-private platform that brings together stakeholders to brainstorm and push the development of charging infrastructure and new zero-emission mobility policies in the country
- Zero-emission vehicles have registration and road tax exemptions
- Zero-emission vehicles enjoy discounted tax rates for the private use of company cars
- Netherlands has established extensive public charging network, with 0.8 public charging points per electric passenger vehicle at the end of 2015
- Netherlands introduced the Open Charge Point Interface (OCPI) protocol to support the national agreement on interoperability of charge points
- National Knowledge Platform for Charging Infrastructure launched in the country, supporting research and development to attain economies of scale for public charging infrastructure manufacturing
- Green Deal Initiative introduced to increase publicly accessible electric charging infrastructure
- Local government such as in Amsterdam and Utrecht, have also come up with a number of incentives such as EV purchase subsidy, establishment of low emission zones, exclusive parking permits, public and private transport fleet electrification, charging stations powered by renewable

energy sources, research and development in EV space by local universities, etc.

Electric mobility is developing at a rapid pace

The global electric car fleet exceeded 5.1 million in 2018, up by 2 million since 2017, almost doubling the unprecedented amount of new registrations in 2017. China remained the world's largest electric car market with nearly 1.1 million electric cars sold in 2018 and, with 2.3 million units, it accounted for almost half of the global electric car stock. Europe followed with 1.2 million electric cars and the United States with 1.1 million on the road by the end of 2018 and market growth of 385000 and 361000 electric cars from the previous year. Norway remained the global leader in terms of electric car market share at 46% of its new electric car sales in 2018, more than double the second-largest market share in Iceland at 17% and six-times higher than the third-highest Sweden at 8%.

Electric two/three-wheelers on the road exceeded 300 million by the end of 2018. The vast majority are in China. With sales in the tens of millions per year, the Chinese market for electric two-wheelers is hundreds of times larger than anywhere else in the world. In 2018, electric buses continued to witness dynamic developments, with more than 460000 vehicles on the world's road, almost 100000 more than in 2017.

In addition to conventional passenger vehicles, low-speed electric vehicles (LSEVs) in 2018 were estimated at 5 million units, up almost 700000 units from 2017. All LSEVs were located in China. Shared "free floating" electric foot scooters flourished very rapidly in 2018 and early 2019 in major cities around the world. These foot scooter schemes now operate in around 129 cities in the United States, 30 in Europe, 7 in Asia and 6 in Australia and New Zealand.

In freight transport, electric vehicles (EVs) were mostly deployed as light-commercial vehicles (LCVs), which reached 250000 units in 2018, up 80000 from 2017. Medium truck sales were in the range of 1000-2000 in 2018, mostly concentrated in China.

The global EV stock in 2018 was served by 5.2 million light-duty vehicle (LDV) chargers, (540000 of which are publicly accessible), complemented by 157000 fast chargers for buses. The number of EV chargers continued to rise in 2018 to an estimated 5.2 million worldwide for light-duty vehicles (LDVs). Most are slow chargers (levels 1 and 2 at homes and workplaces), complemented by almost 540000 publicly accessible chargers (including 150000 fast chargers, 78% of which are in China). With the 156000 fast chargers for buses, by the end of 2018 there were about 300000 fast chargers installed globally.

The global EV fleet consumed an estimated 58 terawatt-hours (TWh) of electricity in 2018, similar to the total electricity demand of Switzerland in 2017. Two-wheelers continued to account for the largest share (55%) of EV energy demand, while LDVs witnessed the strongest growth of all transport modes in 2017-18. China accounted for 80% of world electricity demand for EVs in 2018. The global EV stock in 2018 emitted about 38 million tonnes of carbon-dioxide equivalent (Mt CO_2-eq) on a well-to-wheel basis. This compares to 78 Mt CO_2-eq emissions that an equivalent internal combustion engine fleet would have emitted, leading to net savings from EV deployment of 40 Mt CO_2-eq in 2018.

Policies have major influences on the development of electric mobility

Policy approaches to promote the deployment of EVs typically start with a vision statement and a set of targets. An initial step is the adoption of electric vehicle and charging standards. Procurement programmes kick-start demand and stimulate automakers to increase the availability of EVs on the market, plus provide impetus for an initial roll out of publicly accessible charging infrastructure. Another useful policy measure is to provide economic incentives, particularly to bridge the cost gap between EVs and less expensive internal combustion engine (ICE) vehicles as well as to spur the early deployment of charging infrastructure. Economic incentives

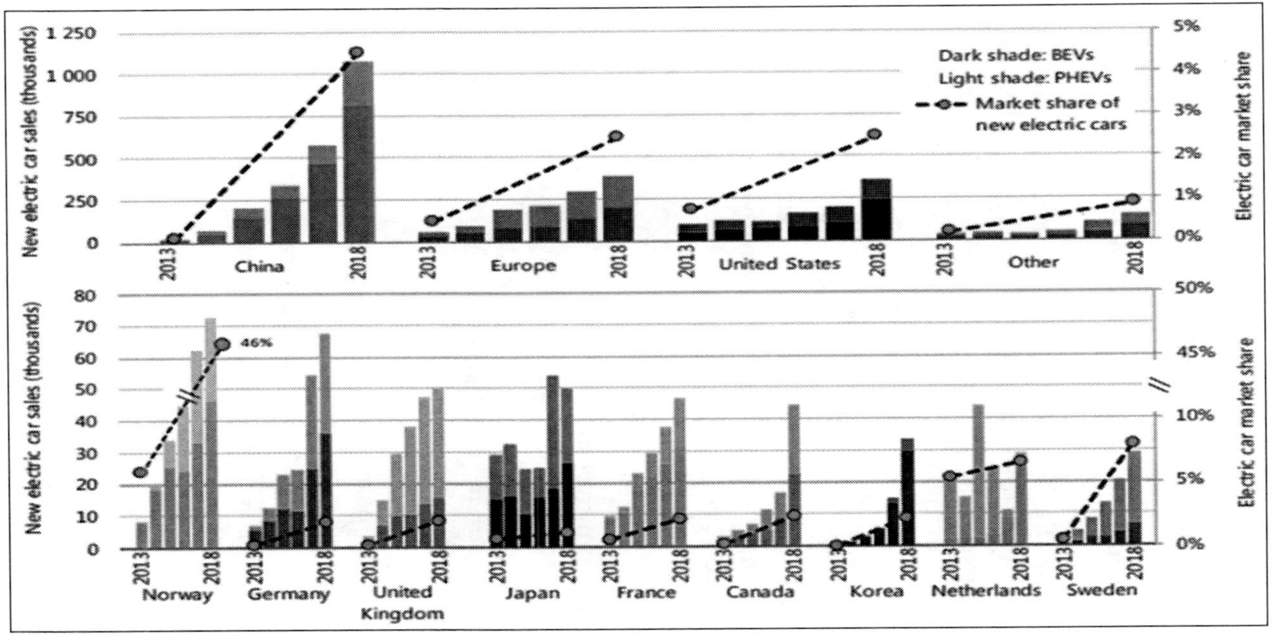

Figure 76: Global electric car sales and market share, 2013-18

Source: IEA analysis based on country submissions

Notes: BEVs = battery electric vehicles; PHEVs = plug-in hybrid electric vehicles. Europe includes Austria, Belgium, Bulgaria, Croatia, Denmark, Estonia, Finland, France, Germany, Greece, Hungary, Iceland, Ireland, Italy, Latvia, Liechtenstein, Lithuania, Luxembourg, Malta, Netherlands, Norway, Poland, Portugal, Romania, Slovakia, Slovenia, Spain, Sweden, Switzerland, Turkey and United Kingdom. Other includes Australia, Brazil, Chile, India, Japan, Korea, Malaysia, Mexico, New Zealand, South Africa and Thailand.

are often coupled with other policy measures that increase the value proposition of EVs (such as waivers to access restrictions, lower toll or parking fees) which are often based on the better performance of EVs in terms of local air pollution. Measures that provide crucial incentives to scale up the availability of vehicles with low and zero tailpipe emissions include fuel economy standards, zero-emission vehicle mandates and the rise in the ambition of public procurement programmes. Regulatory measures related to charging infrastructure include minimum requirements to ensure "EV readiness" in new or refurbished buildings and parking lots, deployment of publicly accessible chargers in cities and on highway networks, and are complemented by requirements regarding inter-operability and minimum availability levels for publicly accessible charging infrastructure. So far only observed in Norway, when the EV and charging infrastructure deployment evolves, some policy measures may need to be adjusted as the markets and infrastructure mature. One example is how fuel and vehicle taxes are adjusted and their contribution to government revenue.

Front running countries such as those involved in the Electric Vehicles Initiative are already making progress from their initial phases of EV policy implementation (e.g. establishment of standards, public procurement and early charging roll out, economic incentives). Many of these countries have regulatory instruments in place and, to date, some advanced markets like Norway have started phasing out some aspects of their EV support policies.

Table 4: EV-related policies in selected regions

		Canada	*China*	*European Union*	*India*	*Japan*	*United States*
Regulations (vehicles)	ZEV mandate	✓*	✓				✓*
	Fuel economy standards	✓	✓	✓	✓	✓	✓
Incentives (vehicles)	Fiscal incentives	✓	✓	✓	✓		✓
Targets (vehicles)		✓	✓	✓	✓	✓	✓*

		Canada	China	European Union	India	Japan	United States
Industrial policies	Subsidy	✓	✓			✓	
Regulations (chargers)	Hardware standards**	✓	✓	✓	✓	✓	✓
	Building regulations	✓*	✓*	✓	✓		✓*
Incentives (chargers)	Fiscal incentives	✓	✓	✓		✓	✓*
Targets (chargers)		✓	✓	✓	✓	✓	✓*

* Indicates that the policy is only implemented at a state/province/local level.

** Standards for chargers are a fundamental prerequisite for the development of EV supply equipment. All regions listed here have developed standards for chargers. Some (China, European Union, India) are mandating specific standards as a minimum requirement, others (Canada, Japan, United States) are not.

Notes: ZEV = Zero-emissions vehicle. Check mark indicates that the policy is set at national level. Building regulations refer to an obligation to install chargers in new and renovated buildings. Incentives for chargers include direct investment and purchase incentives for both public and private charging.

Key policy developments in 2018/19 include:

- In the European Union, several significant policy instruments were approved. They include fuel economy standards for cars and trucks and the Clean Vehicles Directive which provides for public procurement of electric buses. The Energy Performance Buildings Directive sets minimum requirements for charging infrastructure in new and renovated buildings. Incentives supporting the roll-out of EVs and chargers are common in many European countries.
- In China, policy developments include the restriction of investment in new ICE vehicle manufacturing plants and a proposal to tighten average fuel economy for the passenger light-duty vehicle (PLDV) fleet in 2025 (updating the 2015 limits). The use of differentiated incentives for vehicles based on their battery characteristics (e.g. zero-emissions vehicle credits and subsidies under the New Energy Vehicle mandate).

- Japan's automotive strategy through a co-operative approach across industrial stakeholders, aims to reduce 80% of greenhouse gas (GHG) emissions from vehicles produced by domestic automakers (90% for passenger vehicles) – including exported vehicles – to be achieved by 2050 with a combination of hybrid electric vehicles (HEVs), BEVs, PHEVs and fuel cell electric vehicles (FCEVs). Fuel economy standards for trucks were revised and an update of fuel economy standards for cars was announced.
- Canada outlined a vision for future EV uptake accompanied by very ambitious policies in some provinces, such as the zero-emissions vehicles (ZEVs) mandate in Quebec (similar to one in California). British Columbia announced legislation for the most stringent ZEV mandate worldwide: 30% ZEV sales by 2030 and 100% by 2040. This places Canada in a similar framework as the ten states in the United States that have implemented a ZEV mandate.
- India's announced the second phase of the "Faster Adoption and Manufacturing of Electric Vehicles in India" (FAME India) scheme. It reduces the purchase price of hybrid and electric vehicles, with a focus on vehicles used for public or shared transportation (buses, rickshaws and taxis) and private two-wheelers.
- In Korea, the scope of national subsidies for all low-carbon vehicle purchases increased from 32 000 vehicles in 2018 to 57 000 in 2019, adding to other policy instruments including public procurement, subsidies and rebates on vehicle acquisition taxes, reduced highway tolls and public parking fees). An ambition to scale up overseas sales of low-emission vehicles produced in Korea was also announced in 2018. It is accompanied by a goal to boost production capacity to more than 10% of all vehicles by 2022, and the use of financial support and loan guarantees to major industrial players.

Growing momentum on the policy front is also emerging in

other countries. Key examples include Chile, which has one of the largest electric bus fleets in the world after China. Chile's aim is to electrify 100% of its public transport by 2040 and 40% of private transport by 2050. New Zealand also has high ambitions and has adopted a transition to a net-zero emissions economy by 2050. Both New Zealand and Chile joined the Electric Vehicles Initiative (EVI) in 2018.

Policies are crucial to ensure that electric mobility has positive impacts for flexibility in power systems. The use of EVs to provide flexibility services is a feature that has relevant implications to increase opportunities for the integration of variable renewable energy in the electricity generation mix and to reduce costs associated with the adaptation of the grid to increased EV uptake. This requires that power markets evolve in such a way as to include services (e.g. grid balancing) suitable for EV participation and to allow the participation of small loads for demand-side response through aggregators. The update of the European directive on common rules for the internal market in electricity, adopted in March 2019 by the European Parliament as part of the Clean Energy for All Europeans package, is an important milestone in this respect.

Strategic importance of the battery technology value chain is increasingly recognized:

Policy support has been extended to the development of manufacturing capacity for automotive batteries. This reflects the dynamic development of battery technologies and the importance of EVs to achieve further cost reductions in battery storage for a multitude of applications. It also recognizes the strategic relevance that large-scale battery manufacturing can have for industrial development (due to the relevance of its value chain in the clean energy transition). Examples of policy measures related to battery manufacturing include:

- In China, policy support aims to stimulate innovation and induce consolidation among battery manufacturers, giving preference to those that offer batteries with the best performance.

- In the European Union, the Strategic Action Plan for Batteries in Europe was adopted in May 2018. It brings together a set of measures to support national, regional and industrial efforts to build a battery value chain in Europe, embracing raw material extraction, sourcing and processing, battery materials, cell production, battery systems, as well as reuse and recycling. In combination with the leverage offered by its market size, it seeks to attract investment and establish Europe as a player in the battery industry.
- In countries with a smaller domestic market, as is the case for Japan and Korea, the policy support is to reinforce export markets.

In all regions, increasing attention is being given to solid state batteries. This is representative of the rapid pace of innovation in the automotive battery sector. In addition to optimized technical performance, innovation has a pivotal role in economic development. Strengthening capacities for innovation has played a central role in the growth dynamics of successful developing countries.

Outlooks indicate a rising tide of electric vehicles

Dynamic developments in policy implementation and technology advances underpin the projections to 2030 in the New Policies Scenario, which aims to illustrate the consequences of announced policy ambitions. Projections in the EV30@30 Scenario are underpinned by proactive participation of the private sector, promising technology advances and global engagement in EV policy support. It is aligned with the goal of the EVI EV30@30 Campaign to achieve a 30% market share by 2030 for EVs in all modes except two-wheelers (where market shares are higher).

In the New Policies Scenario, China leads with the highest level of EV uptake over the projection period: the share of EVs in new vehicle sales reaches 57% across all road transport modes (i.e. two-wheelers, cars, buses and trucks), or 28% excluding two/three-wheelers. It is followed by Europe, where the EV sales share reaches 26% in 2030, and Japan, one of the global leaders in the transition to electric mobility with a 21% EV share of sales in 2030. In North America, growth is particularly strong in Canada (where EV market shares reach 29% by 2030), as well as in California and US states that have adopted zero-emissions vehicle (ZEV) mandates and have stated an intention to continue to improve vehicle fuel economy. Other parts of the United States are slower to adopt EVs, bringing the overall EV sales share to 8% of the US vehicle market in 2030.

In the EV30@30 Scenario, EVs make up 70% of all vehicle sales in China in 2030 (42% excluding two/three-wheelers). Almost half of all vehicles sold in 2030 in Europe are EVs, 37% in Japan, more than 30% in Canada and United States, 29% in India and 22% in other countries, taken together.

The electric car targets announced by automobile manufacturers align closely with the stock projections in the New Policies Scenario in 2020. In 2025, the auto industry targets range between the projections of the New Polices Scenario and of the EV30@30 Scenario.

Expansion of automotive battery manufacturing capacity will largely depend on the evolution of electrification in car markets. This is due to the number of electric cars sold that far exceeds sales volumes of other modes (except two-wheelers), and the size of their battery packs, which are much larger for cars than for two-wheelers. There is growing consensus that the electrification of cars will be a pivotal pillar to reduce unit cost of automotive battery packs. Thanks to their instrumental role to facilitate the availability of energy storage at lower costs, EVs are also likely to be a crucial step for the transition to a cleaner energy system.

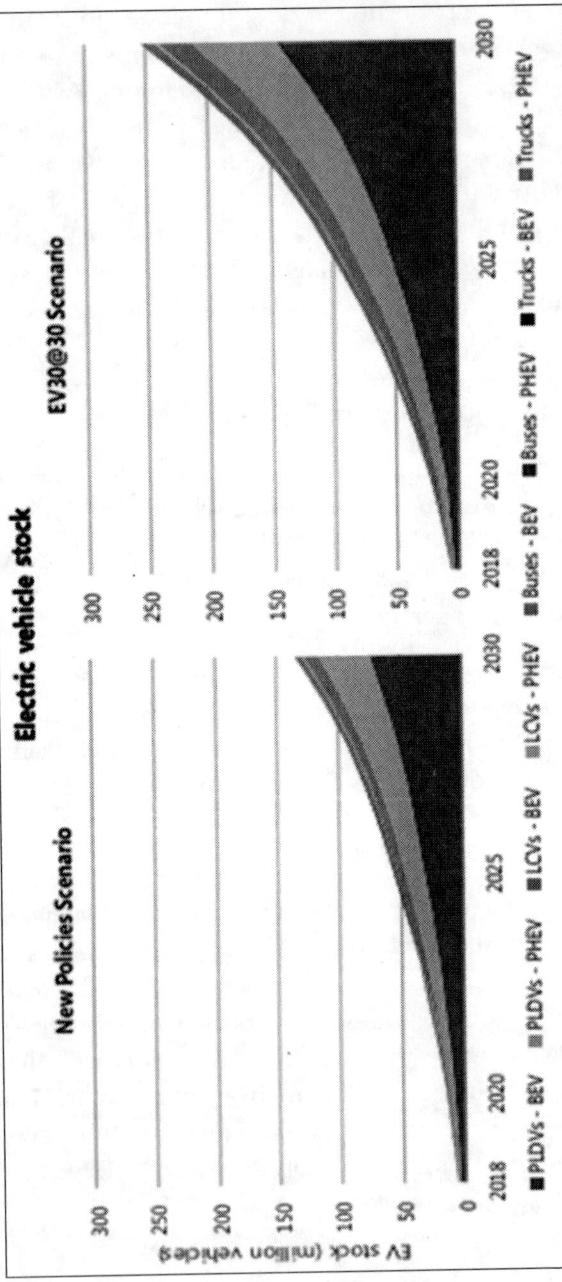

Figure (Contd.)

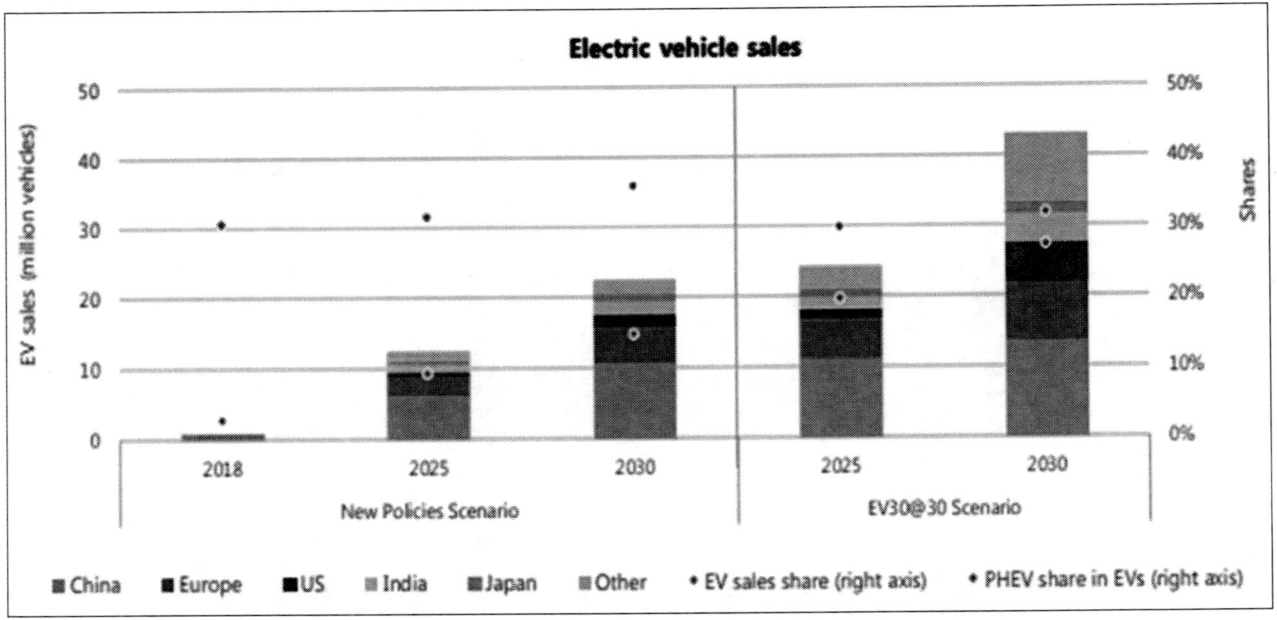

Figure 77: Future global EV stock and sales by scenario, 2018-30

Source: IEA analysis developed with the IEA Mobility Model

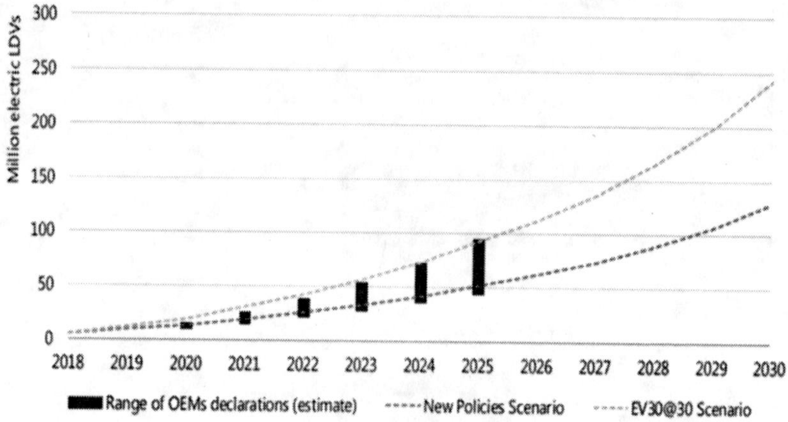

Figure 78: Projected global electric car stock compared with OEM targets (2020-25)

Note: The cumulative sales shown in this figure are based on OEMs announcements on the number of EVs deployed in a target year and then extrapolating these values for the following years using a range of assumptions. The number of electric vehicles deployed by each OEM in its target year is calculated taking into account three possible inputs: i) an absolute target value of EV sales given by an OEM, ii) a target value expressed in terms of models deployed, iii) a targeted percentage of the OEM sales.

EV electricity demand and save energy

Electricity demand projected in both scenarios suggests that EVs are going to be much more relevant for power systems than they have been in the past. With uncontrolled charging, EVs could drive incremental needs for peak power generation and transmission capacity. Understanding the extent to which power systems can be impacted depends on total annual electricity demand EVs, the impact of daily charging patterns on load profiles, location power levels used for charging.

Slow chargers (mostly private LDV chargers) account for more than 60% of the total electricity consumed globally to charge EVs in both the New Policies and the EV30@30 scenarios (shares differ region-by-region, as they depend on the extent of the uptake of EVs across transport modes). This is beneficial to power system

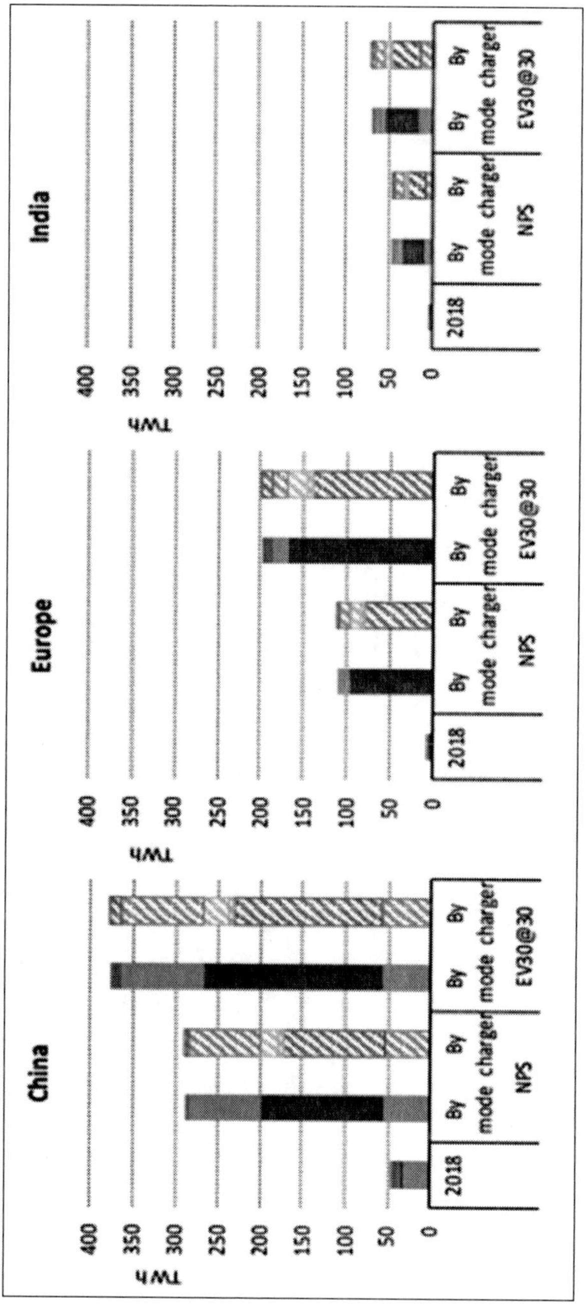

Figure 79

(Contd.)

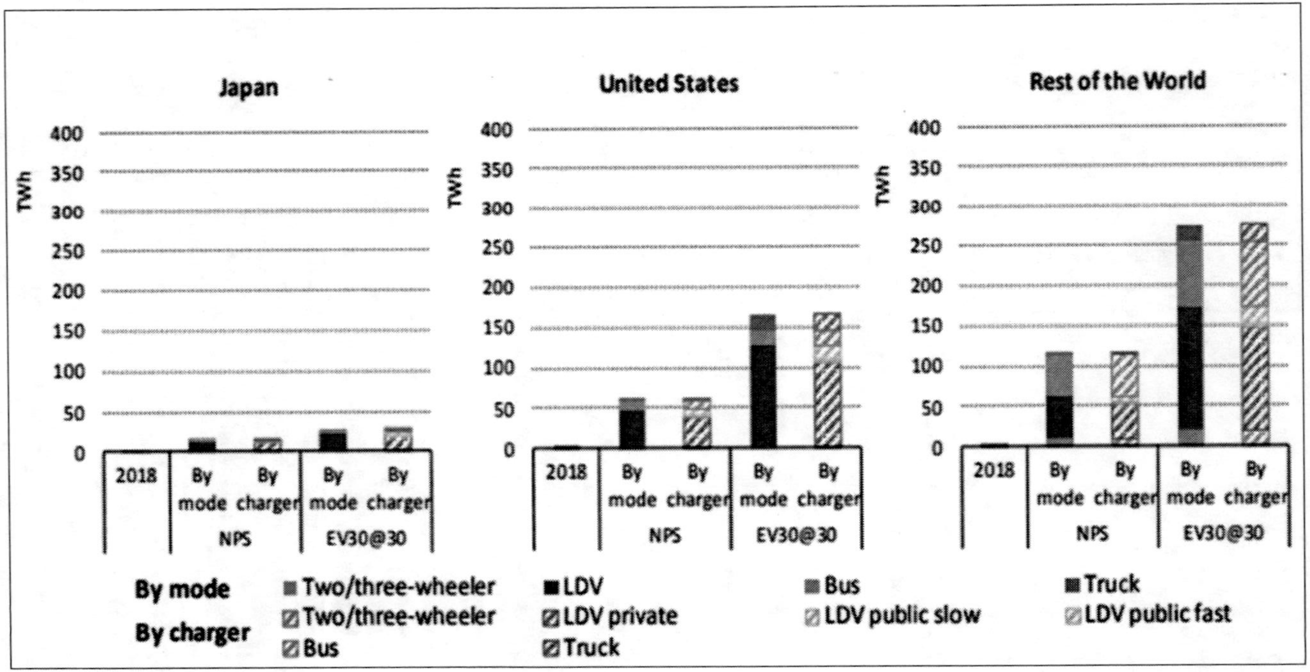

Source: IEA analysis developed with the IEA Mobility Model

Notes: NPS = New Policies Scenario, EV30@30 = EV30@30 Scenario, LDV = light-duty vehicle

management, since slow charging comes with opportunities for EVs to provide flexibility services to power markets, provided that controlled EV charging is in place. As fast charging demand is highest for buses in both scenarios, concentrating these charging events at night when electricity demand is lower could help flatten the overall shape of a power demand curve.

Controlled EV charging is well suited to contribute to increased flexibility in power systems. This feature has positive implications for the increasing contribution of variable renewable energy in a power generation mix and can also address grid stability issues. Features include:

- EVs can minimize impacts on load profiles of power systems by managing their charging patterns to coincide with low demand periods.
- EVs have potential to provide ultra-short-term demand response to a power system when required (e.g. frequency control), leverage the properties of EV batteries to allow very fast and precise response to control signals, as well as the ability to shift demand across time periods.
- EV batteries can store energy that may be used for other purposes than powering the vehicle, thanks to the opportunities offered by vehicle-to-grid and similar technologies (e.g. vehicle-to-home).

Electricity markets should facilitate the provision of ancillary services such as grid balancing in which EVs are among the potential participants, and allow for the participation of small loads through aggregators. To participate in demand response in the electricity market, it is important to minimize the transaction costs (including not only fees, but also other regulatory, administrative or contractual hurdles) to make it easier for aggregators to pool small loads.

Vehicles –

Light-duty vehicles

In 2018, the dynamic developments on the policy front continued to be mirrored by announcements from automakers on their electrification strategies, even beyond what had been observed in previous years.

Table 5: OEM announcements related to electric cars

Original equipment Manufacturer	*Announcement*
BMW	15-25% of the BMW Group's sales in 2025 and 25 new EV models by 2025
BJEV-BAIC	0.5 million electric car sales in 2020 and 1.3 million electric car sales in 2025
BYD	0.6 million electric car sales in 2020
Chonquing Changan	21 new BEV models and 12 new PHEV models by 2025, 1.7 million sales by 2025 (100% of group's sales)
Dongfeng Motor CO	6 new EV models by 2020 and 30% electric sales share in 2022
FCA	28 new EV models by 2022
Ford	40 new EV models by 2022
Geely	1 million sales and 90% of sales in 2020
GM	20 new EV models by 2023
Honda	15% electric vehicle sale share in 2030 (part of two-thirds of electrified vehicles by 2030, globally and by 2025 in Europe)
Hyundai-Kia	12 new EV models by 2020
Mahindra & Mahindra	0.036 million electric car sales in 2020
Mazda	One new EV model in 2020 and 5% of Mazda sales to be fully electric by 2030
Mercedes-Benz	0.1 million sales in 2020, 10 new EV models by 2022 and 25% of the group's sales in 2025
Other Chinese OEMs	7 million sales in 2020
PSA	0.9 million sales in 2022
Renault Nissan Mitsubishi	12 new EV models by 2022. Renault plans 20% of the

Original equipment Manufacturer	*Announcement*
	group's sales in 2022 to be fully electric. Infiniti plans to have all models electric by 2021
Maruti Suzuki	A new EV models in 2020, 35 000 electric car sales in 2021 up to 1.5 million in 2030
Tesla	Around 0.5 million sales in 2019 and a new EV model in 2030
Toyota	More than ten new models by the early 2020s and 1 million BEV and FCEV sales around 2030
Volkswagen	0.4 million electric car sales in 2020, up to 3 million electric car sales in 2025, 25% of the group's sales in 2025, 80 new EV models by 2025 and 22 million cumulative sales by 2030
Volvo	50% of group's sales to be fully electric by 2025

German OEMs were among the most far reaching in their statements regarding the intention to embrace vehicle electrification. In March 2019, Volkswagen announced they would consider leaving the German car industry association Verband der Automobilindustrie (VDA) in the absence of a change to concentrate more efforts on battery electric cars (Welt, 2019). Shortly thereafter, BMW and Daimler agreed that electric mobility will be one of the central technologies in the coming decade to comply with environmental legislation in the European Union and that VDA will work towards a consensus paper as the basis for the expansion of the charging infrastructure as well as future funding schemes (Murphy, 2019).

In Japan, Toyota stated its intention is to continue investing in hydrogen-fuelled vehicles and releasing new models (Tajitsu and Shiraki, 2018).

Some of the OEMs that are leading the way in vehicle electrification opted to share technologies and platforms with other manufacturers. For example, Volkswagen announced that it is willing to share its new EV platform [the Modular Electric Toolkit (MEB)] with others (Volkswagen, 2019a). Similarly, Toyota announced that it will share its hybrid technology patents with other OEMs (Omoto, 2019), a move that resembles the one made by Tesla in 2014 (Tesla, 2014). This can be interpreted as a way to hedge against the risk of taking a major technology initiative in isolation from other manufacturers and therefore as something that increases chances of wider consumer awareness and buy-in for the new technology. In the case of Volkswagen, sharing the technology platform would also help all OEMs to reach economies of scale faster. Overall, increased co-operation among manufacturers is likely to accelerate the technological transition to electric mobility.

As a result of these announcements, the number of electric car models available is expected to increase significantly in the coming years, diversifying the products available. It shows the distribution of BEV and PHEV models in 2018 and beyond in the three main global electric car markets – China, Europe and United States – classified by passenger car segment. It illustrates that China will remain ahead of other regions in terms of model availability. It also indicates that BEVs and PHEVs will be subject to a more homogeneous introduction across all passenger car segments, with the main exception of PHEVs in the small vehicle segment.

Two/three-wheelers

The production of electric two-wheelers has been centered in China and focused mainly on low speed and short-range vehicles (see Chapter 1, Small electric vehicles for urban transport). However the market is beginning to move towards electrification of two wheelers with performance characteristics (speed in particular) that are compatible with competing ICE technologies.

Part of this change can be attributed to new players. The Chinese company NIU, which sold 290000 electric scooters in 2018, entered joined the stock market and is expanding its sales to Europe and North America (NIU, 2019). Another important new player is Gogoro, which is based in Chinese Taipei but is present in Europe as well (Box 2.3). Govecs, an electric scooter start-up in Europe

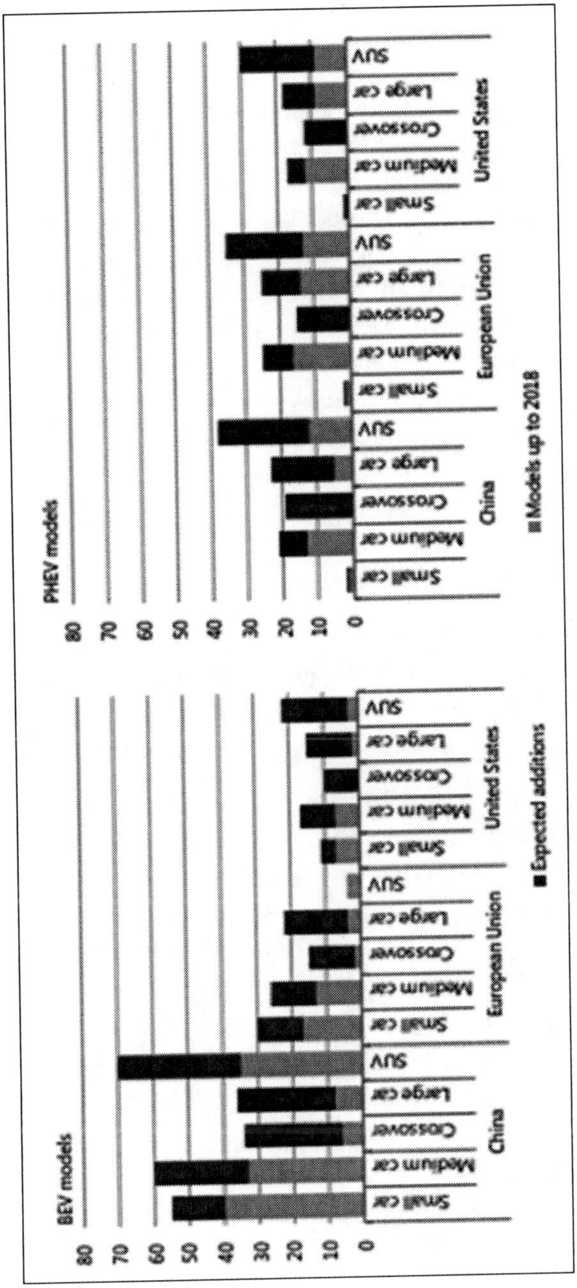

Figure 80: Electric car models available: 2018 and expected additions

Source: EV volumes 2019.

with around 15 000 sales annually, is rapidly expanding and will soon join the stock market.

Incumbent manufacturers are also joining the electric two-wheeler market: BMW, Honda, Peugeot and Piaggio all have at least one electric model in their line-up. In India, the main two wheeler manufacturer, Hero Moto Corp, offers seven electric models. Ducati and Harley Davidson, premium motorcycle companies, have announced ambitious electrification plans. The technical specifications of premium two-wheelers are very high as all-electric range of 100-200 km is not uncommon. It is interesting to note, that in premium electric scooters, regenerative braking is becoming a common feature, thus further reducing their energy consumption.

Buses

Most activity in the electric bus market is in China and the largest key players in this field are:

Chinese OEMs. During 2018, policy action and increased interest in bus electrification spread widely across other regions relative to previous years. Notable leading developments include:

- In Europe, BYD, a Chinese manufacturer, started production at its second European battery factory (in France) and is supplying buses to the United Kingdom (BYD, 2018). Alfabus, also a Chinese manufacturer, began supplying its products in Italy. Today at least three major Chinese OEMs are offering their models on the European market (BYD, Yutong and Alfabus). European OEMs including Daimler, Scania, Solaris, MAN, VDL, Volvo, and Iveco continue to increase their electric bus supply (Transport & Environment, 2018).
- In the FAME Phase II scheme in India, the ambition to promote the electrification of public transportation includes an aim to deploy 7 000 buses (Cabinet of India, 2019). Co-operation between Indian and Chinese OEMs has started.

For example, Olectra Greentech Limited (formerly Goldstone) and BYD are producing electric buses for India with a target to manufacture 5000 units annually by March 2021. Other Indian OEMs such as Tata Motors and Ashok Leyland have taken steps to increase production or introduce new models.

- The three main suppliers of electric buses in North America are BYD (Chinese), New Flyer (Canadian) and Proterra (United States). Both BYD and New Flyer have announced increased investments in electric bus factories in the United States (CleanTechnica, 2018; Mass Transit, 2018). Proterra has received investment by Daimler with the aim of jointly developing electric school buses (Proterra, 2018).
- In other regions, electric buses are being supplied by Chinese OEMs including BYD, Sunwin Bus Corporation, Yutong, Zhongtong Bus, Higer Bus and King Long. This is the case for several cities in Chile and Colombia, and a few others in Latin America (China Dialogue, 2019). In Australia, companies such as Yutong and Zhongtong have also begun trials for some routes (Australasian Bus & Coach, 2019).

Trucks

In 2018, OEMs announced ambitious plans to electrify their product lines and some of the first models have become commercially available. Significant plans to electrify medium- and heavy-duty vehicles have been announced by DAF, Daimler, MAN, Navistar, Nikola, PACCAR, Volkswagen and Volvo. 32 Emerging OEMs such as Tesla and Thor Trucks and others have joined incumbent OEMs with their announcements to roll out production (Kolodny and Petrova, 2018; Tesla, 2019).

Efforts are concentrated around the electrification of medium-duty trucks that are mostly used for urban delivery or waste collection. These categories are the most favourable for electrification due to relatively short driving range requirements (around 200 km). All OEMs with electric ambitions have announced at least one model for this segment and models by Daimler and BYD are commercially available. Some of these announcements (including Navistar – together with Volkswagen, Thor Trucks and Tesla) relate to the introduction of electric medium- to long-haul trucks. Longer range BEV trucks have been announced by Tesla and Freightliner, both class 8 trucks with electric ranges of 480-960 km. The Tesla Semi is in commercial testing and market introduction is expected as early as 2019. It focuses on freight vehicles with a long driving range, which excludes terminal vehicles and service vehicles for street cleaning or waste collection.

Automotive batteries

It is estimated that approximately 70 gigawatt-hours (GWh) of battery cells were produced for electric LDVs in 2018. Production is concentrated in China, which accounts for over 50% global market share, with the rest being split between the United States, Korea and Japan. There are currently around 60 manufacturers in China with the top-two companies, BYD and CATL, accounting for more than half of the Chinese market. To reap the benefits of economies of scale, battery manufacturing is moving to increase manufacturing capacity. Even if the majority of production still is sourced from small plants (3-8 GWh/year capacity), several recent announcements of production capacity expansion point to an increase in plant size as well as new entrants in the automotive battery market, adding to increases in capacity utilization rates of existing plants. Each of the three biggest battery factories currently in operation, all recently built, have a capacity of 20 GWh/year and account for roughly 21% of the total installed capacity. Most of these are located in China, Japan and Korea.

Eight plants with a capacity of more than 20 GWh/year are expected to be in production by 2023. In total, these will have a production capacity of more than 180 GWh/year, almost 2.5-times more than LDV battery production in 2018. In the longer term, plants with capacities around 100 GWh are being discussed.

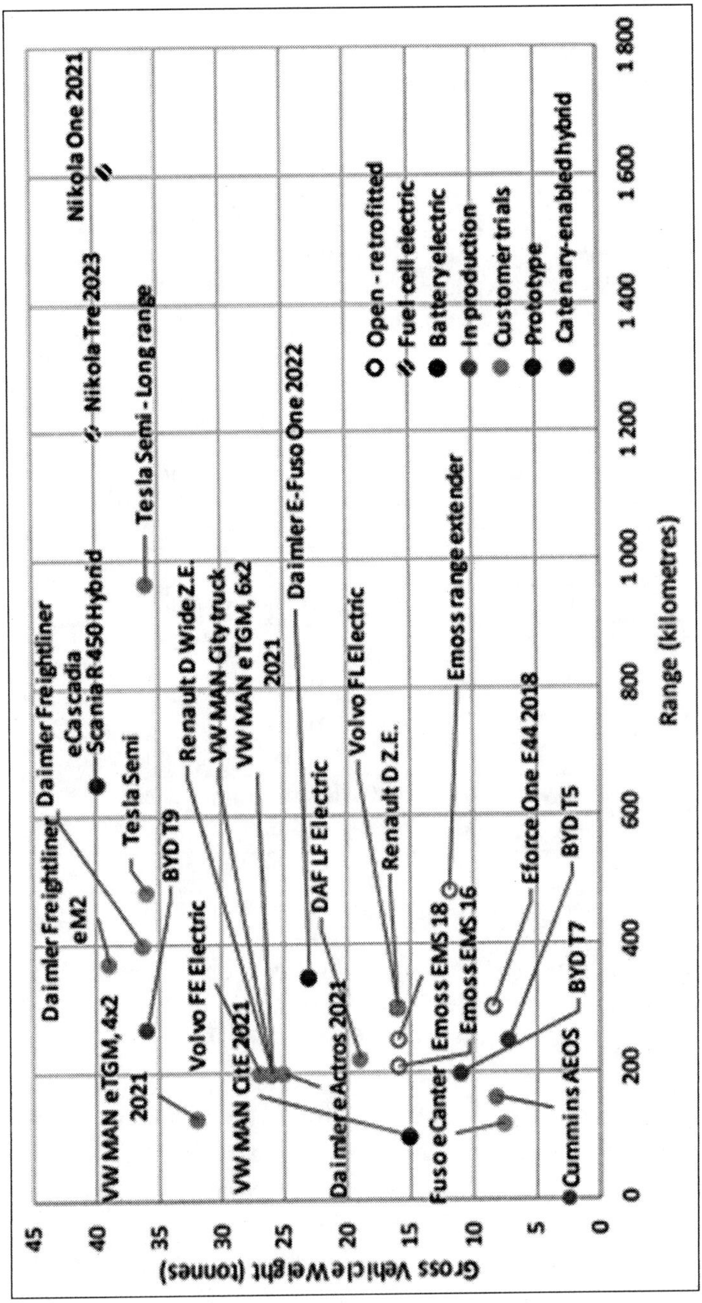

Figure 81: Heavy-duty electric truck models announced for commercialization

Panasonic considered expanding production (to 105 GWh/year) at its Gigafactory, but the expansion plans were suspended in April 2019 (Lambert, 2018). CATL has spoken about the possibility of expanding its Erfurt plant to up to 100 GWh/year (Hetzner, 2019).

Announced battery manufacturing facilities

OEM	*Country*	*Announcements*
Panasonic	United States	35 GWh/year factory by 2020
CATL	China	24 GWh/year and 18 GWh factories in 2020
	European	14 GWh/year factory in 2021
	Union	98 GWh/year factory (date to be determined) to be launched
BYD	China	24 GWh/year factory in 2019.20 GWh/year and 30 GWh factories in 2023.10 GWh/year factory (date to be determined)
LG Chem	European Union	15 GWh/year factory in 2022
	China	32 GWh/year factory in 2023
SK innovation	China	7.5 GWh/year factory in 2020
	European Union	7.5 GWh/year factory in 2021
	United States	9.8 GWh/year factory in 2022
LIBCOIN/BHEL	India	30 GWh/year factories, in 2025, 2026 and 2027
Samsung SDI	European Union	1.65 GWh/year factory in 2020
Northvolt	European Union	32 GWh/year factory in 2023
Lithium Werks	China	8 GWh/year factory in 2021
Terra E	European Union	4 GWh/year factory in 2020

The market for battery cells has been characterized by overcapacity in recent years and this appears to still be the status. This was favored by tax exemptions available to electric cars under the New Energy Vehicle Subsidy Programme (Government of China, 2018). Investment in battery manufacturing in China also came from foreign companies. Major examples include LG Chem, which is investing over USD 1 billion to expand their battery production in Nanjing (LG Chem, 2018), and Panasonic, which at its Dalian plant in 2018 started producing over 5 GWh/year. Lithium

Werks, a European battery company, also announced the construction of an 8 GWh/year factory (Lithium Werks, 2018). Foreign investments in battery manufacturing in China may be explained by two factors. First, factories in China can be used for export to other markets. Second, if the announced phase-out of the New Energy Vehicle Subsidy Programme in 2020 is maintained, it can open a large market for all battery manufacturers.

Capacity of automotive batteries

The EV deployment described in the Outlook section of this chapter is facilitated by increases in battery capacity. The extent to which this increase materializes does not only depend on the magnitude of future EV sales, but also on the balance between various electric powertrains, given that they are equipped with different battery capacities and on the future size of the batteries. Today battery pack sizes differ across regions and vehicle models. In all main markets, battery pack capacity in BEVs has been increasing in recent years, from 20-30 kilowatt-hours (kWh) in 2012 to 35-70 kWh in 2018. The upward trend is most pronounced in the United States, where a rapid shift to cars with large batteries (mostly Tesla) is additional to the broader increase of battery capacity in other models. Battery size for PHEVs is approximately 10-13 kWh in most regions, a value compatible with roughly 50-65 km of all electric driving range.

The capacities of batteries have increased to provide longer driving distances. In the future, the observed trend towards larger battery pack sizes is expected to continue until most BEVs have a driving range of at least 350-400 km. This means battery capacities of 70-80 kWh for BEVs, while PHEVs are expected to have battery capacities of about 10-15 kWh in 2030. Similar factors may drive battery capacities for LCVs to increase from the current range of 35-90 kWh to around 100 kWh, and for BEVs and from about 10 kWh to around 20 kWh for PHEVs in 2030.

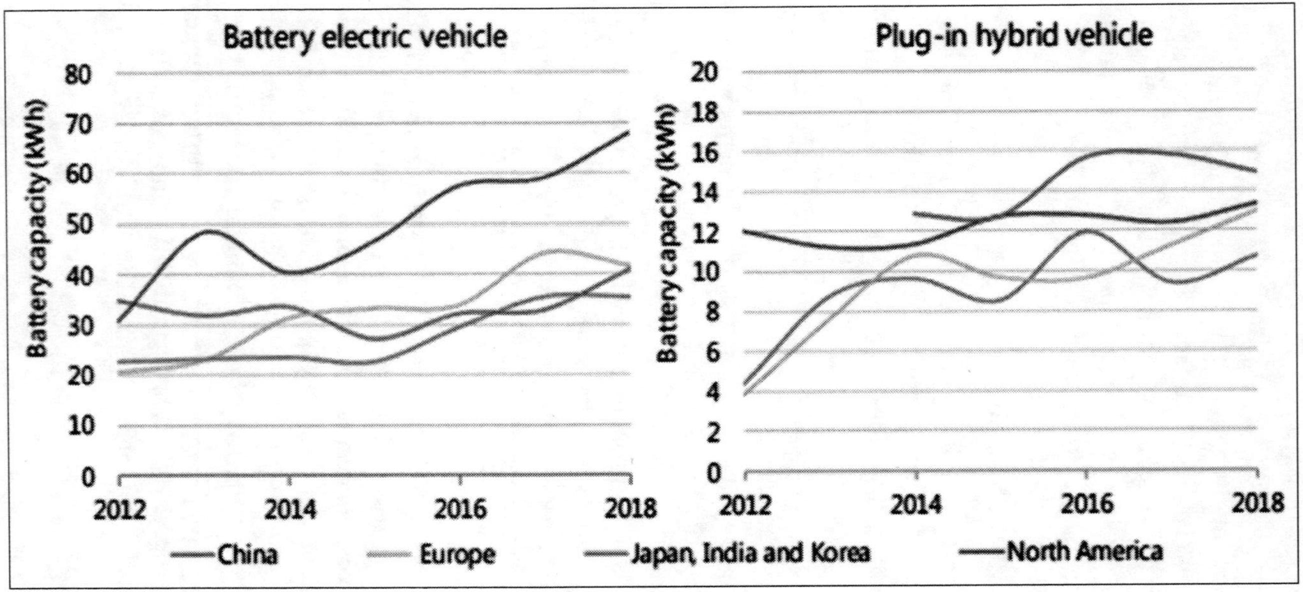

Figure 82: Battery pack capacities of BEVs and PHEVs in key regions, 2012-18

Sources: Data for 2012-15 are based on IHS Markit (2019), 2016-17 on Marklines (2019) and 2018 on EV Volumes (2019)

The expansion of battery manufacturing capacity will largely depend on the evolution of electrification in the car market. This means that the electrification of cars will be a crucial pillar of the reduction of the unit cost of automotive battery packs.

In the EV30@30 Scenario, the surge of global battery capacity is faster and reaches a higher level in 2030, around 2.8 TWh/year. This is attributable both to the higher EV sales projected for this scenario and the higher share of BEVs. As in the New Policies Scenario, LDVs represent almost 90% of the total battery capacity in 2030, with battery electric cars alone accounting for 82% of the total.

Material demand for automotive batteries

The expansion of annual battery production projected in both the New Policies Scenario and the EV30@30 scenario leads to significantly higher demand for materials to manufacture batteries.

Bigger EV battery capacity implies increased demand for new materials in the automotive sector. The nature of the material demand will vary according to the development of battery chemistry. The cathode chemistries of automotive lithium-ion battery packs are transitioning towards higher nickel content to provide higher energy density. Information on the current mix of chemistries is not fully consistent across various data providers, but there is broad consensus that the main chemistries currently in use are LFP, NCA and NMC, with the latter being subject to a transition from NMC 111 to chemistries with lower cobalt content, to manage the risks associated with cobalt supply and to increase energy density.

Charging Infrastructure

The collection of information on private sector announcements on EV charger deployments made for the Global EV Outlook 2018 focused primarily on the deployment of highway chargers (IEA, 2018). In this edition, we broaden the coverage of the

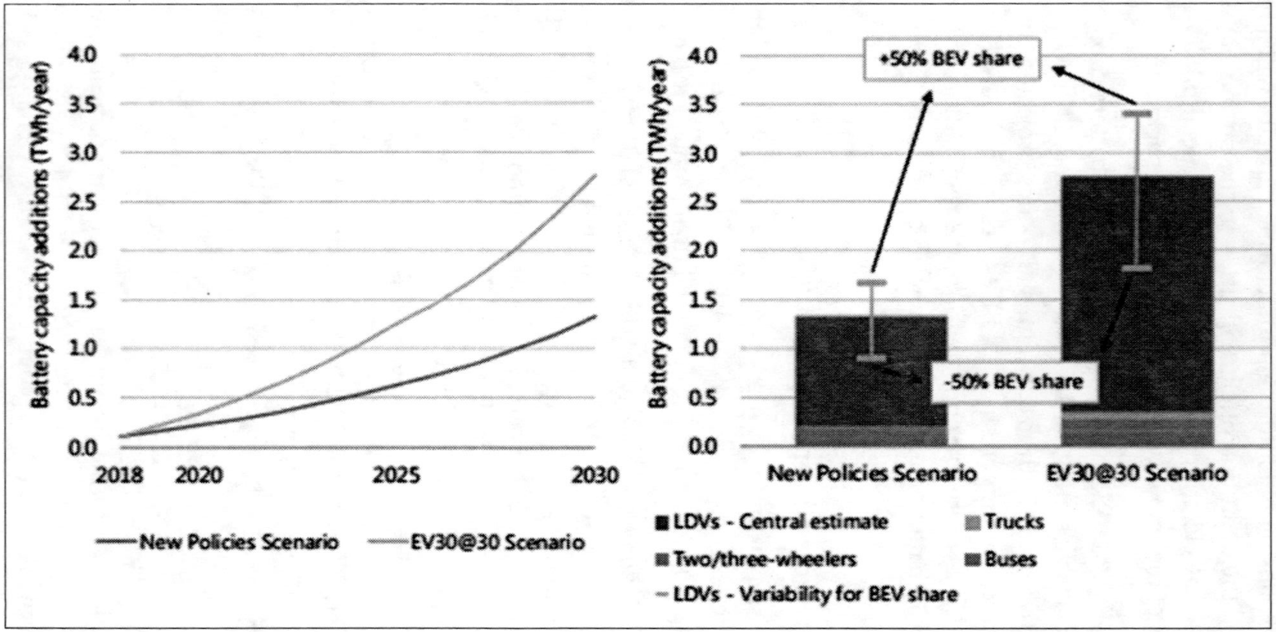

Figure 83: Annual global battery capacity addition for EV sales by scenario, 2018-30

Source: IEA Mobility Model (IEA, 2019)

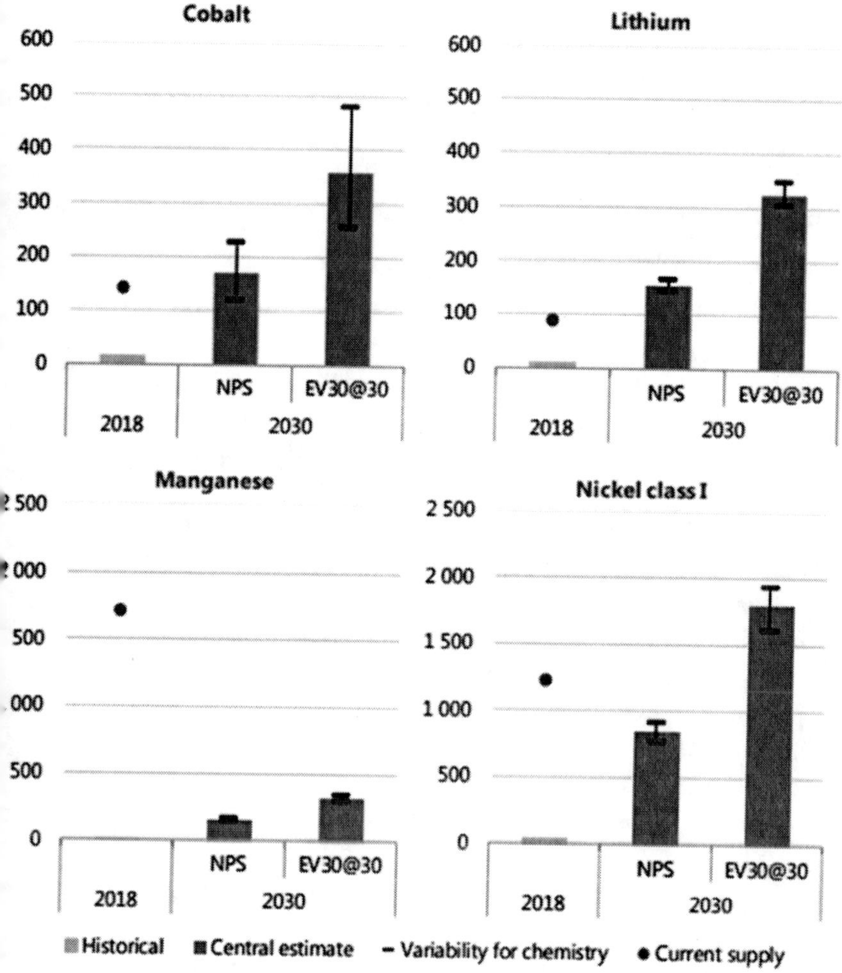

Figure 84: Increased annual demand for materials for batteries from deployment of electric vehicles by scenario, 2018-30

Source: IEA analysis developed with the IEA Mobility Model

announcements to also look at other types of chargers. Expanding the scope of the announcements covered leads to an important challenge, closely related to the information shown in figure. It summarizes announcements on deployment of EV charging infrastructure and categorizes them in three main groups: commitments that relate to all types of chargers, pledges only for publicly accessible chargers, and statements only targeting highway charging infrastructure.

The most significant are announcements by two large operators: Charge Point, the world's largest network of EV charging stations in the United States and Europe (also a supporter of the EV30@30 Campaign) and EV-Box, a provider originally based in the Netherlands and recently acquired by ENGIE, a large company in the power sector. The magnitude of these announcements is boosted by the fact that these operators include private chargers and have a multinational presence. Other large-scale EV charging deployment pledges (including private chargers) are from EDF, a major utility. In addition, Enel X, a subsidiary of Enel, is focusing on services for the power market and scaling up its international presence (primarily in Europe and in South America) and targeting businesses, cities and individuals. In the United States, utilities are active in deploying charging infrastructure in states such as California, New York, New Jersey and Maryland (The National Law Forum, 2018). Various large US utilities are in the phase of pilot projects, such as DTE Energy, Duke Energy and Consumers Energy Company. Utilities are also taking action through infrastructure investment (e.g. upgrading transformers) and deploying smart meters.

Impacts of electric mobility on energy demand

Electricity demand from EVs

As the stock of electric vehicles and their use expands, more electricity will be needed. In the New Policies Scenario, power demand from the global EV fleet is projected to reach almost 640

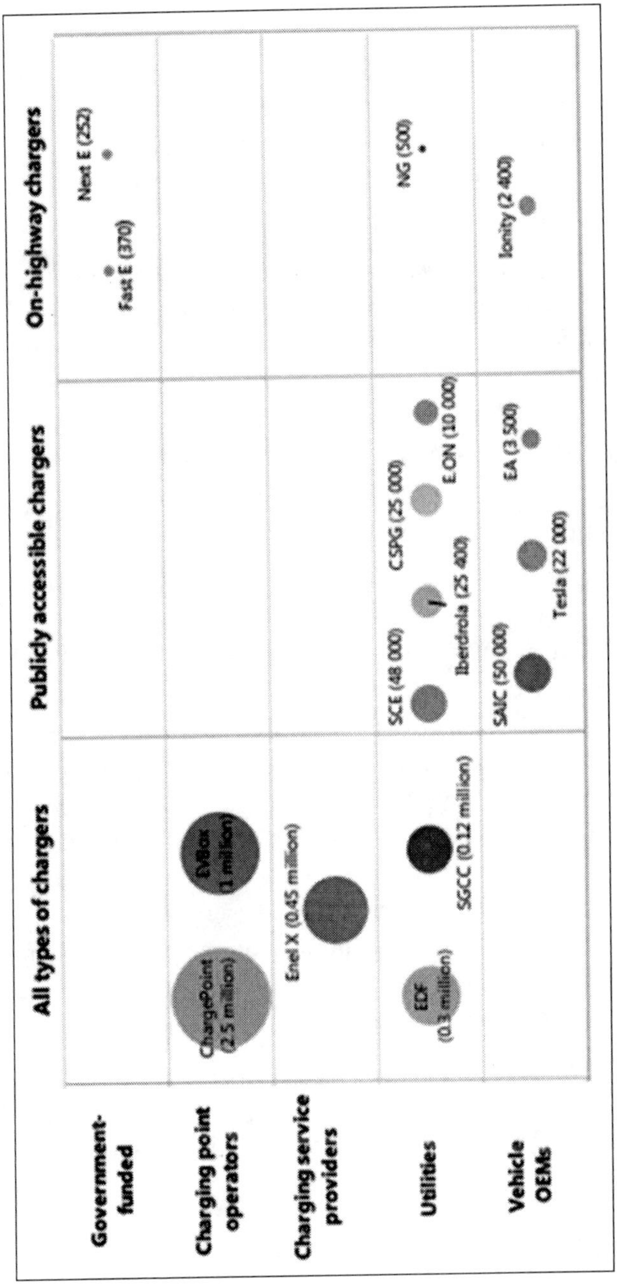

Figure 85: Selected providers of charging infrastructure and recently announced plans/targets

TWh in 2030, about equivalent to the total final electricity consumption in Germany and the Netherlands in 2017. This is a tenfold increase from the 2018 level of 58 TWh. In the EV30@30 Scenario, the larger volume of EVs demands slightly more than 1100 TWh of electricity in 2030, almost double the amount of the New Policies Scenario.

Projected electricity consumed by EVs in both scenarios suggests that EVs are going to be far more significant for power systems than they have been in the past and that they will be a driver of increments in peak power generation and transmission capacity. Assessing the extent to which power systems can be impacted must consider the additional power needed for EVs on an annual basis as well as the daily EV charging profiles, the power rate for chargers and locational considerations.

Figure indicates that slow chargers (particularly private LDV chargers) account for about 60% of total electricity demand to charge EVs in 2030 (shares differ by region reflecting the extent of EV uptake across different transport modes). This helps power system management as slow charging provides opportunities for EVs to enhance flexibility. As fast charging demand is highest for buses, concentrating these charging events at night with depot charging, when both transport and electricity demand are lower, could help flatten the overall shape of the power demand curve. Opportunity charging requires high power draws during the day, so depot charging is likely to have lower impacts on the power system.

Structure of electricity demand for EVs in the New Policies Scenario

In the New Policies Scenario, LDVs are the largest electricity consumer among all EVs in 2030, surpassing two/three-wheelers in 2020. LDVs account for about 60% of the total EV power demand in 2030 (PLDVs account for 81% of total LDVs), followed by buses (26%), two/three wheelers (12%) and trucks (2%).

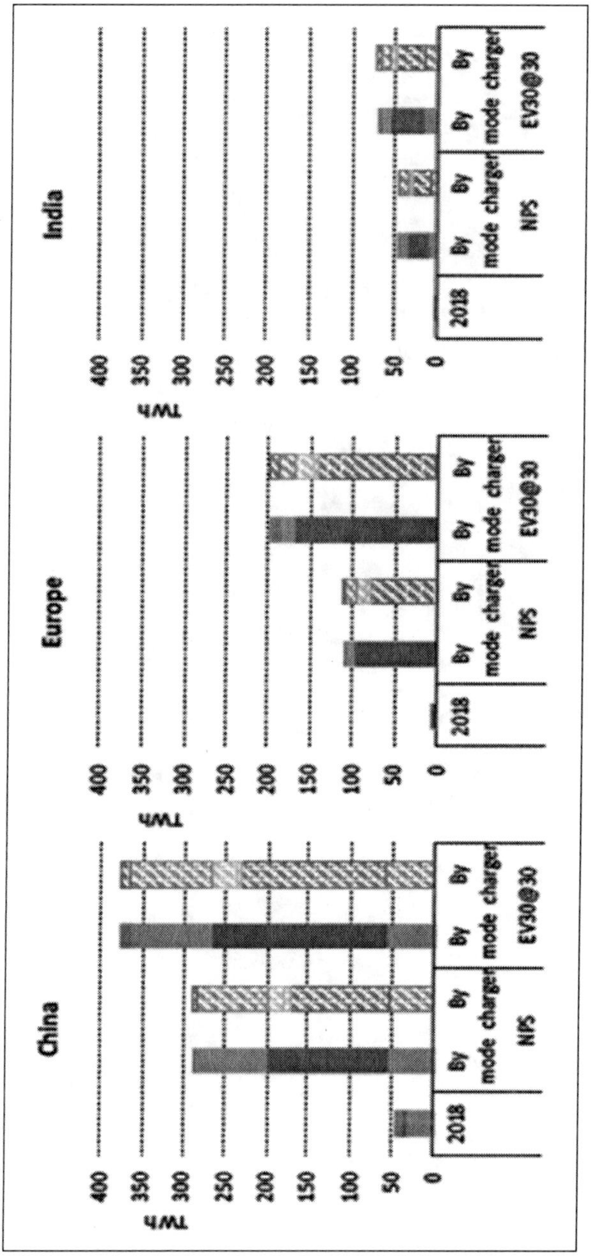

Figure 86

(Contd.)

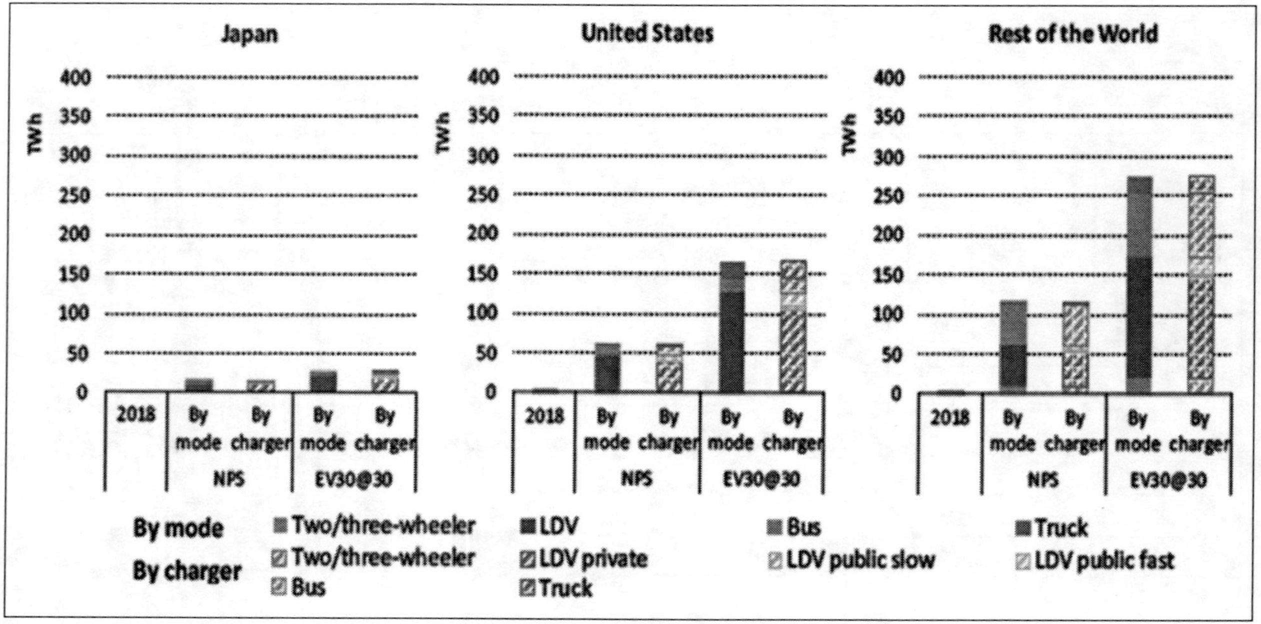

Figure 86: EV electricity demand by region, mode, charger and scenario, 2018 and 2030*

Source: IEA analysis developed with the IEA Mobility Model, 2019

*In the data by type of charger, green and blue colours correspond to slow chargers; red, yellow and orange colours correspond to fast chargers. NPS = New Policies Scenario; EV30@30 = EV30@30 Scenario; LDV = light-duty vehicle

The geographical distribution of power consumption from EVs does not change significantly from today's patterns. China has the highest power demand from EVs throughout the projection period in both scenarios, though its share of total global power demand declines from more than 80% in 2018 to 45% in 2030. China also has the most significant diversification of power demand across modes. In the New Policies Scenario, electricity consumed by EVs in China is about 290 TWh in 2030. Europe at 110 TWh and the United States at 62 TWh follow China in terms of power demand from the EV stock in 2030, corresponding to 17% and 10% of total power demand from EVs. The EV fleets in China and Europe together account for about 62% of total power demand from EVs in 2030. The rest of the world category has the largest increase in power demand from the EV fleet, accounting for 18% of global power demand from EVs in 2030. ASEAN, Canada, Brazil and Korea are responsible for about 45% of the total power demand from the rest of the world category in 2030.

EV fleets make an important contribution to reduce oil use. Globally, the projected EV stock avoids the consumption of 127 million tonnes of oil equivalent (Mtoe) (around 2.5 million barrels/day [mb/d]) of diesel and gasoline in 2030.

Structure of electricity demand for EVs in the EV30@30 Scenario

LDVs account for about 65% and buses for 20% of power demand from EVs in 2030 in the EV30@30 Scenario. This scenario is also characterized by a significant increase in the power demand from trucks (7%), which is almost equivalent to two/three-wheelers (8%) in 2030.

China remains the largest electricity consumer for EVs, despite a further reduction of its share in the global total to 34% in 2030. Europe (18%) of power demand for EVs follows China in this scenario, but the gap with the Unites States (15%) is narrower than in the New Policies Scenario because of the stronger difference in

EV uptake between the scenarios in the case of the United States. In the EV30@30 Scenario, the EV stock displaces 215 Mtoe (4.3 mb/d) of diesel and gasoline in 2030.

Implications of electric mobility for GHG emissions

The evolution of well-to-wheel (WTW) greenhouse has (GHG) emissions from the EV fleet is determined by the combined evolution of the energy used by EVs and the carbon intensity of electricity generation. In 2030 WTW emissions from EVs are lower, with the current and projected carbon intensities of the grid, than those that would result from the continued reliance of ICEs powered by liquid and gaseous fuel blends. The net reduction in WTW emissions from EVs increase, in percentage terms, over time. This reflects expectations in both the New Policies and EV30@30 scenarios of a more rapid decrease in the carbon intensity of electricity generation than in the case of liquid and gaseous fuel blends.

In the New Policies Scenario, the GHG emissions by the EV fleet reach about 230 million tonnes of carbon-dioxide equivalent (Mt CO_2-eq) in 2030. If the projected EVs were driven by ICE powertrains, WTW GHG emissions would almost double (450 Mt CO_2-eq). The global EV fleet in 2030 avoids emissions of about 220 Mt CO_2-eq. In the EV30@30 Scenario, in which the accelerated deployment of EVs is assumed to be coupled with a trajectory for power grid decarbonisation consistent with the IEA Sustainable Development Scenario, the projected EV fleet emits almost 230 Mt CO_2-eq in 2030, while the equivalent ICE powered fleet would emit about 770 Mt CO_2-eq. The rapid decarbonisation of power systems envisioned in the EV30@30 Scenario is important to limit the increase of GHG emissions from the rapid growth in the EV stock. Without the decarbonisation of electricity supply, WTW GHG emissions from the EV fleet in the EV30@30 Scenario would be about 340 Mt CO_2-eq by 2030. In the New Policies Scenario, WTW emissions increase 5% while the EV stock increases 93% in 2030. Moreover, Figure shows that in the EV30@30 Scenario after 2020,

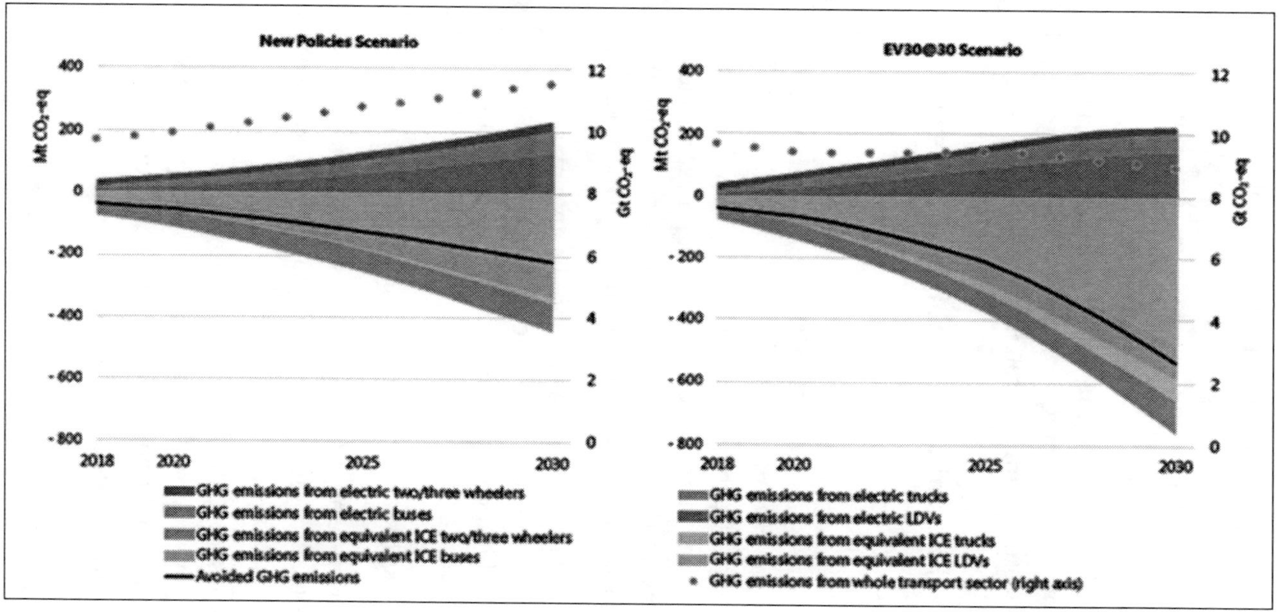

Figure 87: Well-to-wheel net and avoided GHG emissions from EV fleets by mode and total GHG emissions from the transport sector, 2018-30

Sources: IEA analysis developed with the IEA Mobility Model (IEA, 2019), carbon intensities from (IEA, 2018).

total WTW emissions from the transport sector stabilize at around 9.4 Gt CO_2-eq and then decrease to 9 Gt CO_2-eq in 2030, which is more than 20% lower than in the New Policies Scenario.

Despite the comparative advantage of EVs in terms of GHG emissions identified, it is clear that the benefits of transport electrification on climate change mitigation will be greater if EV deployment is parallel with decarbonisation of power systems.

Supply and value chain sustainability of battery materials

Challenges

The growth of a new major industrial sector inevitably leads to consequences for the material and supply chains. For the automotive sector, a transition from ICE vehicles to batteries and electric motors as the main components of the powertrain leads to structural change in the materials used. Challenges surrounding the supply chain of these materials will also gain in importance.

It is important that governments and the auto manufacturing industry develop the needed capacity to anticipate the risks associated with these changes and design strategies to manage them.

The main risks of raw or refined material supply are:

- Production-related (e.g. lack of reserves or resources, 18 under-investment in production capacity, lead times for new capacity).
- Economic (demand/supply balance, including demand fluctuations and sudden disruptions, stockpiling, policies affecting production or import/export options).
- Geopolitical (highly dependent on national policies and strategies, and often exacerbated in cases of geographical concentration of extraction and/or refining).

- Social (impact on the well-being of communities at all scales, local, regional, national and transnational).
- Environmental (e.g. local pollution, supply chain related carbon dioxide (CO_2) emissions, impact on local ecosystems and water resources, landscape destruction).

The future demand for materials for automotive sector will depend on the speed of the transition to electric mobility, as well advances in battery technology and chemistry. The materials needed in the largest quantities for battery packs using the most common battery chemistries are aluminium, graphite/carbon, copper, nickel, cobalt and manganese. An electric car contains about five-times more copper than an equivalent ICE car (ANL, 2018), as it is present in the battery, electric motor and wiring. Copper will also be needed in large quantities for power grid upgrades and infrastructure extensions for electric vehicle charging.

An issue that makes the sustainability of material supply chains difficult to ensure is the lack of identification and traceability of each stakeholder along the material value chains, from the mine to the end-product manufacturer, the OEM in the case of electric vehicles (IEA, 2018). Their international nature and the diversity of local regulations and minimum reporting standards do not help to gain a clear view of the overall value chain. Gaps in the supply chain traceability lead to under-awareness of the social, environmental, corruption and conflict-related risks and hazards associated with each step of the value chain. The limited information for product manufacturers and their customers that results from these gaps in traceability of supply chain does not encourage action.

Battery end-of-life management

The fate of batteries at their end-of-life also has an impact on the sustainability of the material value chain. Different options (some of which can be combined) exist at the end-of-life of the battery as electricity storage on-board of the vehicle. They are broadly grounded on the reuse and recycle components of the wider

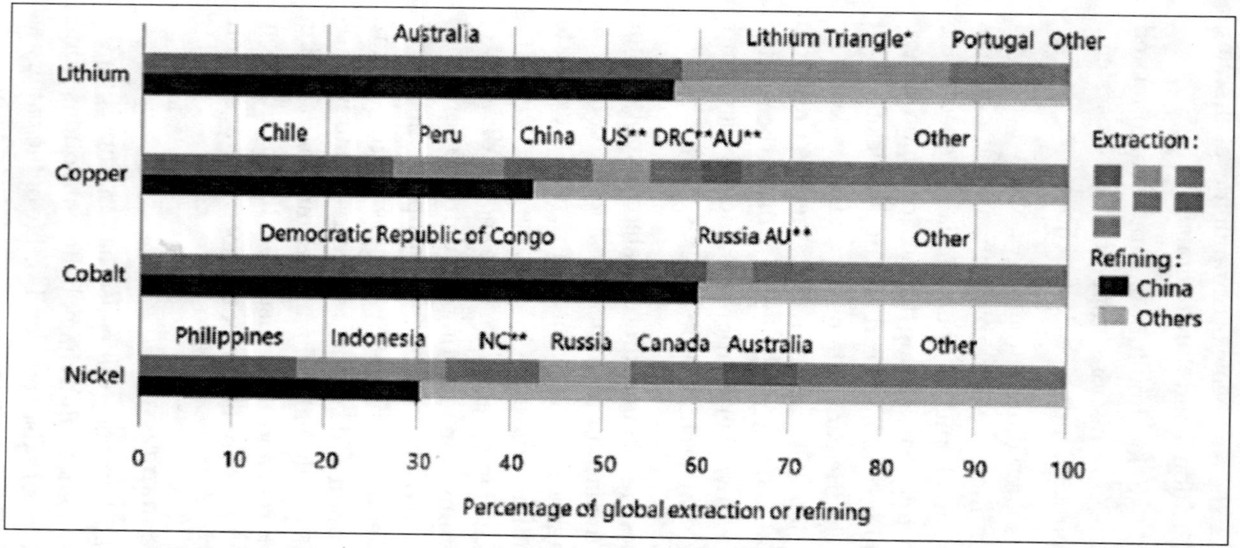

Figure 88: Main extraction and refining locations of key materials for automotive batteries

Sources: USGS 2019, CDI (2016), Sun et al. (2017)

* Lithium Triangle = Argentina, Bolivia and Chile.

** US= United States; AU= Australia; DRC= Democratic Republic of Congo; NC= New Caledonia.

Notes: For extraction, all countries are reported based on 2017 data. For refining, data are based on 2015, 2016 or 2017 depending on the source. Each of the countries aggregated under other have lower material extraction or refining rates than the countries individually presented.

framework on waste prevention, as key alternatives to landfilling. Such end-of-life treatments fall within the circular economy, which ensures that products are kept in use. In terms of battery materials, it enables limiting shortage risks and the dependency on primary raw materials that could be related to potential risks depicted in the table.

Advantages and drawbacks of the main recycling processes suitable for EV batteries

Name of recycling process	*Description*	*Advantages*	*Drawbacks*
Pyro metallurgy	Metals are recovered via high temperature smelting. Separation done by hydrometal-lurgy	Easy implementation	Energy-intensive smelt-ing. Costly because of high energy use. Production of harmful gases. No recovery of aluminium or lithium
Hydrometallurgy	Acids dissolve ions out of the metallic battery parts (nickel, cobalt, lithium) into a solution from which each metal can be recovered by precipitation or solvent extraction	Low energy process. High recovery rate of battery materials.	High consumption of harmful chemicals (waste acid sludge issues). Long process (chemical reactions)
Direct recycling	Use of physical pro-cessessuch as gravity separation of shredded battery materials	Low energy process	Does not permit recovery of each cathode material separately
Bio metallurgy	Hydrometallurgy based on microbial activity to separate ions	Low energy process. High recovery rate of battery materials. Easily manageablete mperature and pressure requirements	Long process (chemical Reactions relying on microbial activity). Requires bacteria culture

Sources: Gaines (2018); Zheng et al. (2018).

* Recovery of these metals is possible through hydrometallurgy, but it is not economically viable.

Notes: Before each process (excluding pyro metallurgy), the battery is disassembled. This first step allows recovery of some metals such as copper and aluminium. Then the battery (or the rest after dismantling) is shredded (can be included for pyro metallurgy). These processes can be combined to optimize recycling rates. The most widely used processes are currently pyro metallurgy and hydro metallurgy.

In China, a programme called "Interim Measures for the Management of the Recycling and Utilization of Power Batteries for New Energy Vehicles" was established to reduce battery waste. It holds vehicle manufacturers responsible for the end-of-life treatment of the vehicle battery. Furthermore, battery manufacturers are encouraged to design batteries that are easy to dissemble since dismantling is the first major step for each recycling process. They also have to provide the technical details of the battery and its dismantling to the companies they supply. Some measures concern the improvement of the traceability system developed by various stakeholders along the supply chain (Government of China, 2018).

In the European Union, the Battery Directive has set standards for industrial and automotive battery waste management since 2006 including the ban of landfilling and incineration. It mandates companies to collect and recycle them. It fixes a minimum required recycling rate for different types of battery. Nevertheless, this policy was determined based on former battery technologies, when zinc-based batteries were dominant, and lithium-ion (Li-ion) batteries had not yet emerged. To adhere to this regulation, the focus is given to materials for which recycling is cheapest, regardless of its criticality or a view to minimize impacts due to extraction (Tytgat, 2013). With the deployment of EVs, volumes of Li-ion batteries are expected to soar. The legal framework thus would benefit from being strengthened and adapted to take account of the new challenges of the EV transition and associated batteries.

Implications of electric mobility for power systems

Challenges

High EV uptake, with uncoordinated charging, can pose a challenge for power systems if this demand coincides with peak demand periods and pushes the peak demand on a system, which could translate to the need for additional generation capacity. Clustering effects in the increased uptake of EVs can also lead to local overloading of distribution networks, resulting in the need to upgrade the distribution network. This includes the replacement of transformers and reinforcement of lines.

Solutions

Controlled EV charging enables access to a range of solutions for power systems through the provision of demand-side response (DSR) services. In particular:

- EVs can minimize impacts on a power system by shaping the electricity demand pattern through changes in the timing of charging events to low-demand periods.
- EVs have the potential to provide energy into the power system when needed. The properties of EV batteries allow very fast and precise response to control signals, as well as the ability to shift demand across longer time periods. These capabilities enable EVs to provide DSR services to the system across a wide range of time scales and to participate in electricity markets. This is a major advantage EVs have compared with other sources of DSR.
- EV batteries can store energy that may be used for other purposes than powering the vehicle, thanks to the opportunities offered by vehicle-to-grid (V2G) and similar technologies (V2X, for example vehicle-to-home). With V2X, EVs serve as battery storage capacity which can discharge energy to buildings and, more generally, the power grid to maintain system stability. This feature can have significant advantages to address challenges at a local level, avoiding overload on a distribution grid, as well as at the main network level.

Role of EV for various types of flexibility services in power systems

Flexibility Type	*Ultra short-term flexibility*	*Very short-term flexibility*	*Short-term flexibility*	*Medium-term flexibility*	*Long-term flexibility*
Time scale	Sub seconds To seconds	Seconds to Minutes	Minutes to days	Days to weeks	Months to years
Electricity Market	Ancillary services	Ancillary services	Ancillary services, balancing, energy markets	Balancing, energy Markets	Balancing, energy Markets
Power system issue	Ensure system stability (voltage, transient and frequency stability) at high shares of variable (non-synchronous) generation		Meeting more frequent, rapid and less predictable changes in the supply/demand balance	Addressing longer periods of surplus or deficit of power generation, e.g. driven by presence of a specific weather system affecting VRE generation	Balancing seasonal and inter-annual availability of variable generation with power demand; meeting capacity requirements when VRE generation is low
Capability of EVs	Batteries can provide fast frequency response based on a control signal. For smart charging, increase or decrease in demand can be offered. The full EV charging load can be somewhat reduced to provide frequency support		Ability to charge earlier or later across one day or more, or at varying charging speed to better suit the system. V2X could provide system services and help meet system requirements. Aggregated charging capacities of large EV fleets can be part of a virtual power plant (VPP), either through DSR or V2X.		Smart charging helps meet capacity needs by shifting EV demand according to system requirements, and can impact long-term planning of capacity. Aggregated charging capacities of large EV fleets can be part of a VPP.

Source: Adapted from IEA (2018).

Notes: VRE = variable renewable energy. The capability of EVs to contribute to long-term flexibility is complemented by other actions that can take place across the whole power system, for example, including shifts in demand for other electrical devices.

CONCLUSION

The slow down on getting the EV policy out is based on the fact that simultaneously India's policy makers have to address issues that pertain to:

(a) managing the reduction in carbon footprint by having calibrated introduction of renewable energy in charging infrastructure

(b) Addressing the issues that are raised by auto ancillary industry through a gradual approach in introduction of EVs, so that the industry has reaction time to acquire the technology and build the production facilities to services OEMs entering into EV manufacturing.

(c) Alleviating the lopsidedness of the electronic manufacturing in this country and providing fillip for manufacturing of batteries and other components in India, rather than resorting to massive imports.

LIST OF REFERENCES

1. Automotive Components Manufacturers Association's
2. India Leaps Ahead: Transformative Mobility Solutions for All", NITI Aayog—Rocky Mountain Institute Report, May 2017
3. 'Snapshot: Auto Ancillary Industry in India', by e-Research & Publications India Private Limited
4. Society of Indian Automotive Manufactures (SIAM) website
5. India Brand Equity Foundation (IBEF) website
6. "Electric vehicle scenarios for India: Implications for development and mitigation", by PR Shukla, Subash Dhar, and Kalyan Bhaskar Indian Institute of Management, Ahmedabad, India & UNEP Riso Center, Rosskilde, Denmark
7. "India Leaps Ahead: Transformative mobility solutions for all." Report by NITI Aayog and Rocky Mountain Institute, May 2017
8. Electric Vehicle Scenarios and a Roadmap for India, Report by IIM-A and CEPT University
9. Five-part Battery infographic series by Nevada Energy Metals, eCobalt Solutions Inc., and Great Lakes Graphite appeared in visualcapitalist.com
10. "Instantly Rechargeable Battery Could Change the Future of Electric and Hybrid Automibiles" by Purdue University, https://www.purdue.edu/newsroom/releases/2017/Q2/instantly-rechargeable-battery-could-change-the-future-of-electric-and-hybrid-automobiles.html
11. "Air Breathing Battery" by MIT website
12. "Phinergy Aluminum Air Batter Capable Fueling" by Phinergy website

13. "Electric Car Charging 101 – Types of Charging, Charging Networks, Apps & More!" by Zach, September 2015, https://evobsession.com/electric-car-charging-101-types-of-charging-apps-more/
14. "Electric Vehicle Charging Guide" by Charge Hub, https://chargehub.com/en/electric-car-charging-guide.html
15. "Challenges and Solutions to developing India's Electric Vehicle charging infrastructure" by Rajiv Menon and Rajeev Tiwary, November 2017, http://www.firstpost.com/tech/news-analysis/challenges-and-solutions-to-developing-indias-electric-vehicle-charging-infrastructure-4206585.html
16. "Big EV Charging Infrastructure Deals Popping Up In India" by Saurabh Mahapatra, October 2017, https://cleantechnica.com/2017/10/18/nationwide-ev-charging-infrastructure-deal-announced-india/
17. ABB Plans 4,500 EV Charging Sations Across Inida by Saurabh Mahapatra, October 2017, https://cleantechnica.com/2017/10/18/abb-plans-4500-ev-charging-stations-across-india/
18. "The Battery Series, The Evolution of Battery Technololgy, by Jeff Desjardins, June 2016, http://www.visualcapitalist.com/evolution-of-battery-technology/
19. "How Electric Car Batteries Work" by Christopher Lampton, https://auto.howstuffworks.com/fuel-efficiency/vehicles/electric-car-battery.htm
20. "Types of Batteries Used for Electric Vehicles" by Brian Mok, Stanford University (2017)
21. "Timeline: History of the Electric Car" http://www.pbs.org/now/shows/223/electric-car-timeline.html (2010)
22. "Electric Vehicle Charging Infrastructure" European Alternative Fuels Observatory, http://www.eafo.eu/electric-vehicle-charging-infrastructure
23. "EV Charging Infrastructure: The Evolving Business Modles" by Saurabh Bansal (2015), https://www.westmonroepartners.com/Insights/Newsletters/West-News-Energy-and-Utilities-April-2016/EV-Charging-Infrastructure
24. "Wireless Charging: Coming Soon to an Electric Vehicle Near

You" by Julia Pyper (2016), https://www.greentechmedia.com/articles/read/wireless-charging-coming-to-an-electric-vehicle-near-you#gs.dkcjKX8

25. "Electronics import by India to touch $300 billion by 2020: Assocham – NEC", by PTA, The Indian Express
26. "Electronic Goods: Demand set to surpass oil bill by 2020" Market Wrap by ICICI Securities (2015), http://content.icicidirect.com/mailimages/ElectronicsGoods.htm
27. "Electric Vehicles: How will it impact smaller auto component manufacturers?" by Nitin Agrawal, Money Control.com, https://www.moneycontrol.com/news/business/moneycontrol-research/electric-vehicles-how-will-it-impact-smaller-auto-component-manufacturers-2380019.html
28. "Carbon footprint cuts: Electric vehicles set to get big boost from Narendra Modi government; know how it will impact you" by Prasanta Sahu, Financial Express, (July 2017)
29. D.A. Kirsch, The electric vehicle and the burden of history. New Brunswick, New Jersey, and London: Rutgers University Press, 2000.
30. "S0301421510001631(3)."
31. "Electric drive." [Online]. Available: https://www.bosch-mobility-solutions.com/en/products-and-services/passenger-cars-and-light-commercial-vehicles/powertrain-systems/electric-drive/. [Accessed: 21-Apr-2018].
32. "How do electric vehicles work?" [Online]. Available: http://www.electricvehiclesmalta.eu/e-driving/how-do-electric-vehicles-work. [Accessed: 15-Apr-2018].
33. "Electrical Engineering and Technology." [Online]. Available: https://www.electrical4u.com/. [Accessed: 15-Apr-2018].
34. M. Faraday, Fundamentals of electric motors 1. 2017.
35. "The Secrets of Electric Cars and Their Motors: It's Not All About the Battery, Folks - The Drive." [Online]. Available: http://www.thedrive.com/tech/17505/the-secrets-of-electric-cars-and-their-motors-its-not-all-about-the-battery-folks. [Accessed: 20-Apr-2018].
36. Y. Guan, Z. Q. Zhu, I. A. A. Afinowi, J. C. Mipo, and P. Farah,

"Difference in maximum torque-speed characteristics of induction machine between motor and generator operation modes for electric vehicle application," Electr. Power Syst. Res., vol. 136, pp. 406–414, 2016.

37. S. R. Jape and A. Thosar, "Comparison of Electric Motors for Electric Vehicle Application," pp. 12–17, 2017.
38. J. Gupta, "Theory & Performance of Electrical Machines." S.K.Kataria& Sons.
39. X.D. Xue, K.W.E. Cheng, and N.C. Cheung, "Selection of Electric Motor Drives for electric vehicles Selection of Electric Motor Drives for Electric Vehicles," January, 2009.
40. "Inside an Electric Car | HowStuffWorks." [Online]. Available: https://auto.howstuffworks.com/electric-car2.htm. [Accessed: 20-Apr-2018].
41. "BU-1004: Charging an Electric Vehicle – Battery University." [Online]. Available: http://batteryuniversity.com/learn/article/bu_1004_charging_an_electric_vehicle. [Accessed: 15-Apr-2018].
42. A. V Kulkarni, "Review on Regenerative Hydralauic Breaking System With Measurement of Performance By Electronic Vaccum Booster," pp. 99–102, 2016

LIST OF APPENDICES

APPENDIX 1

BUSINESS MODELS IN EV SEGMENT

Conductive Charging or Conventional Charging

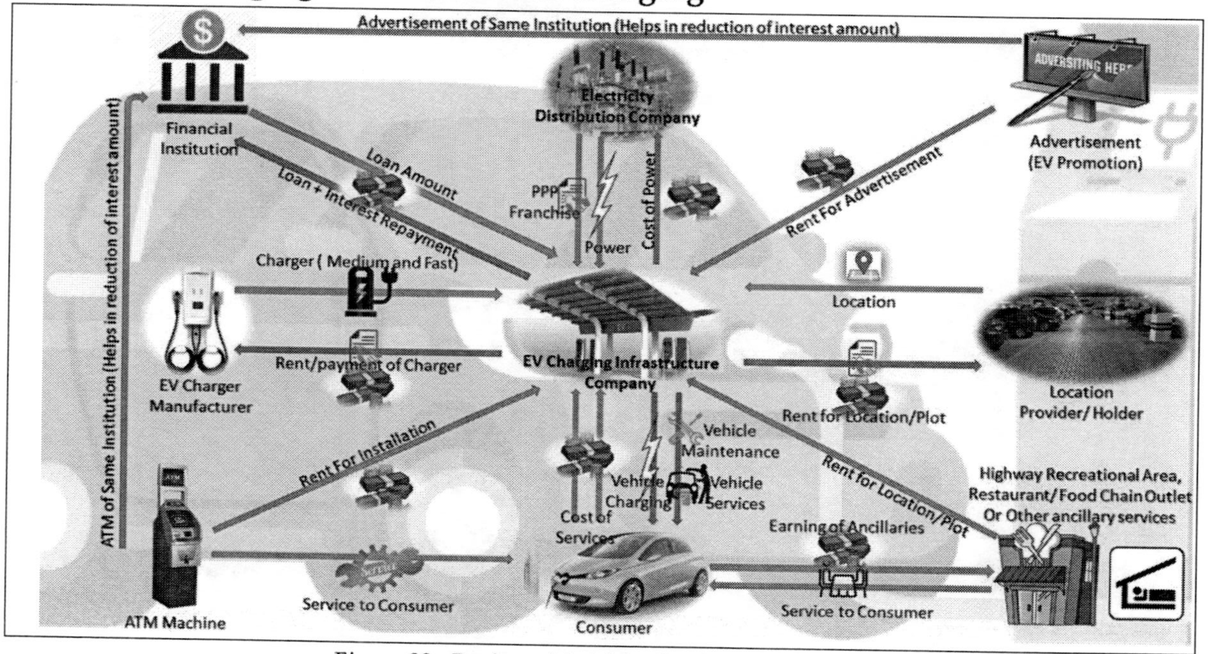

Figure 89: Business Model for Conductive Charging - CapEx

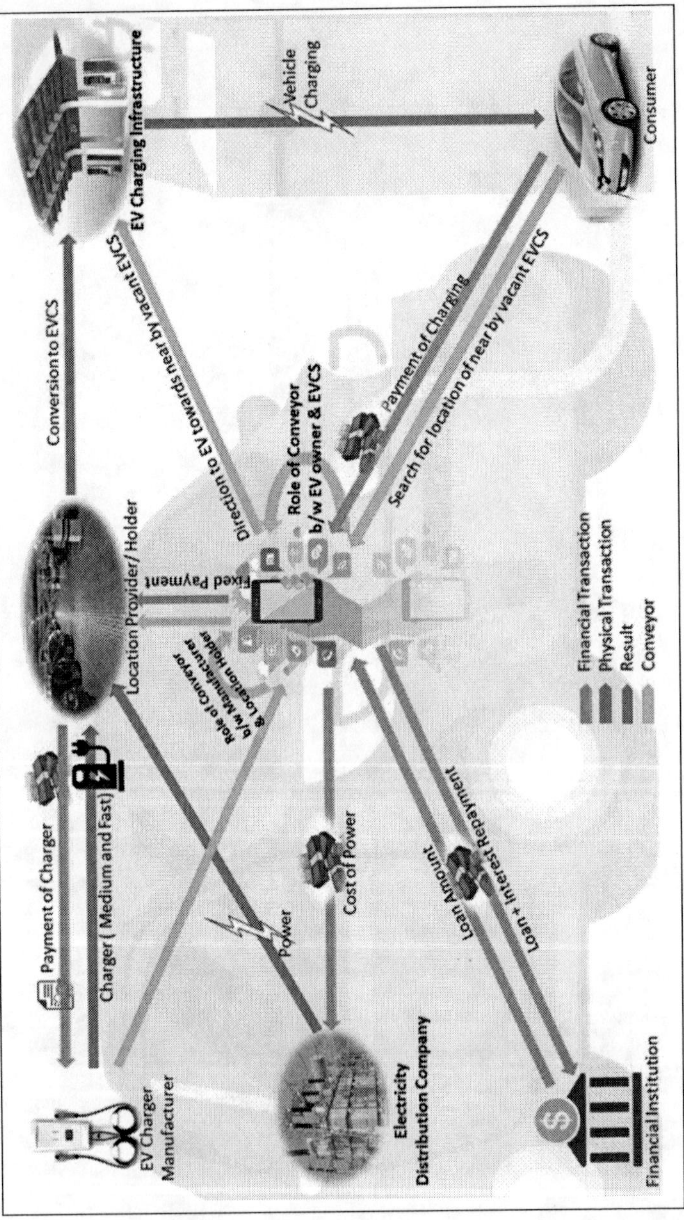

Figure 90: Business Model for Conductive Charging - Aggregrator Model

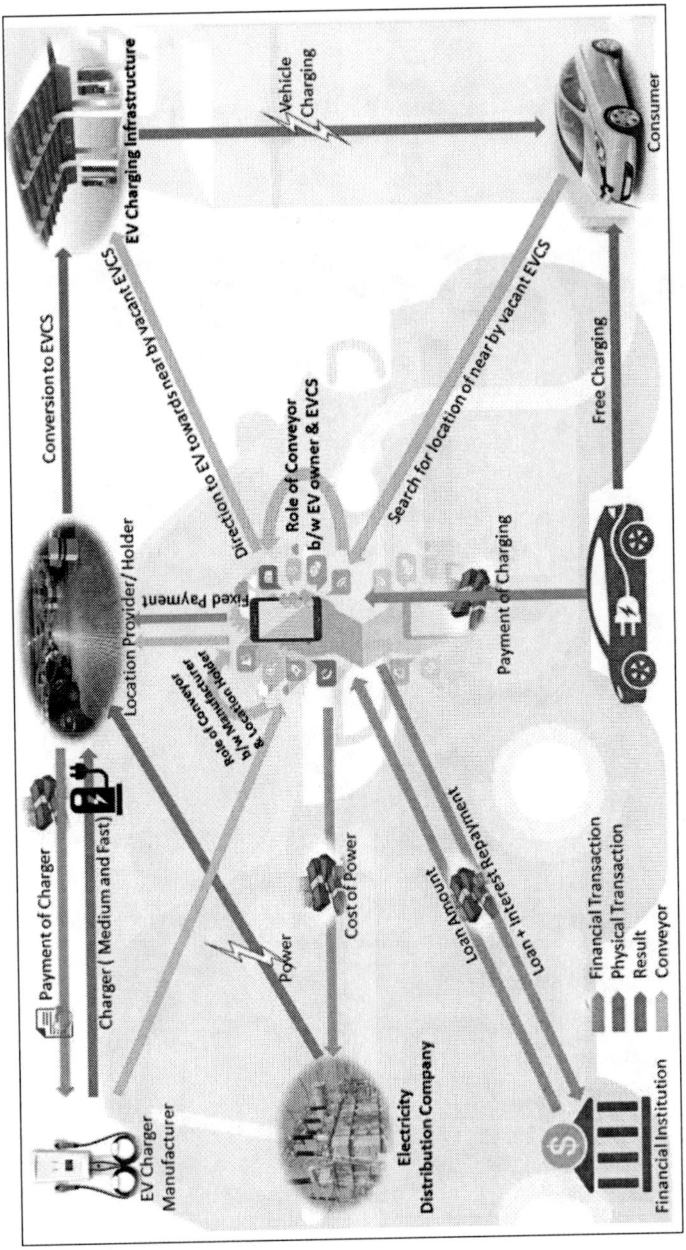

Figure 91: Free Charge Business Model

Inductive Charging or Wireless Charging Business Model

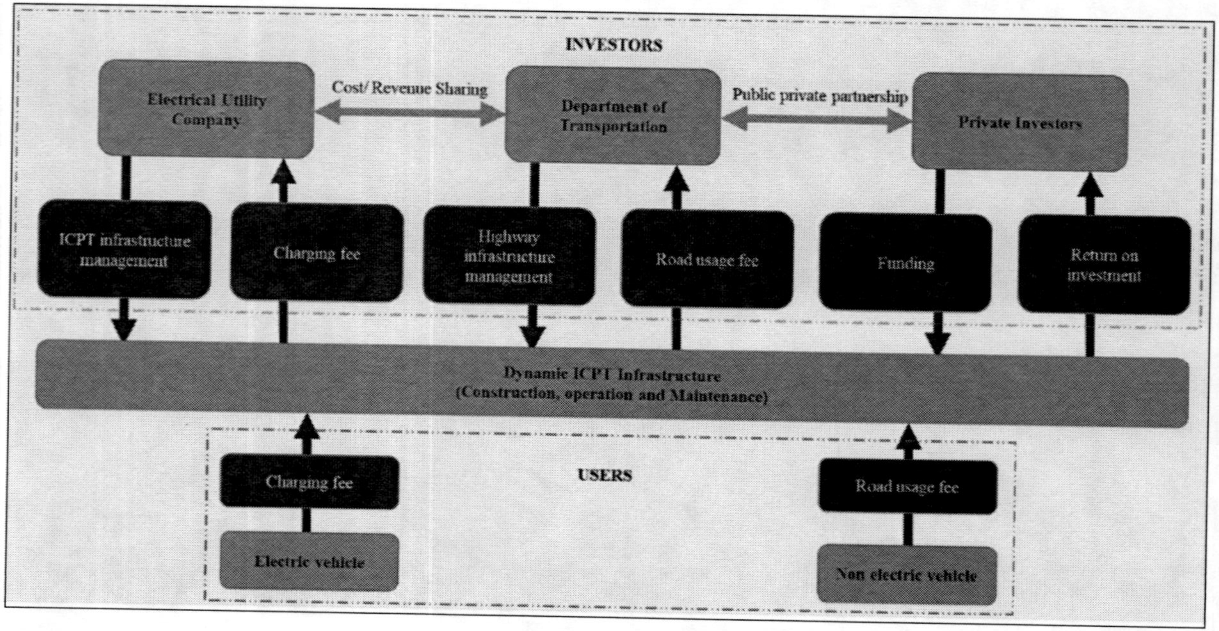

Figure 92: Inductive Charging Business Model

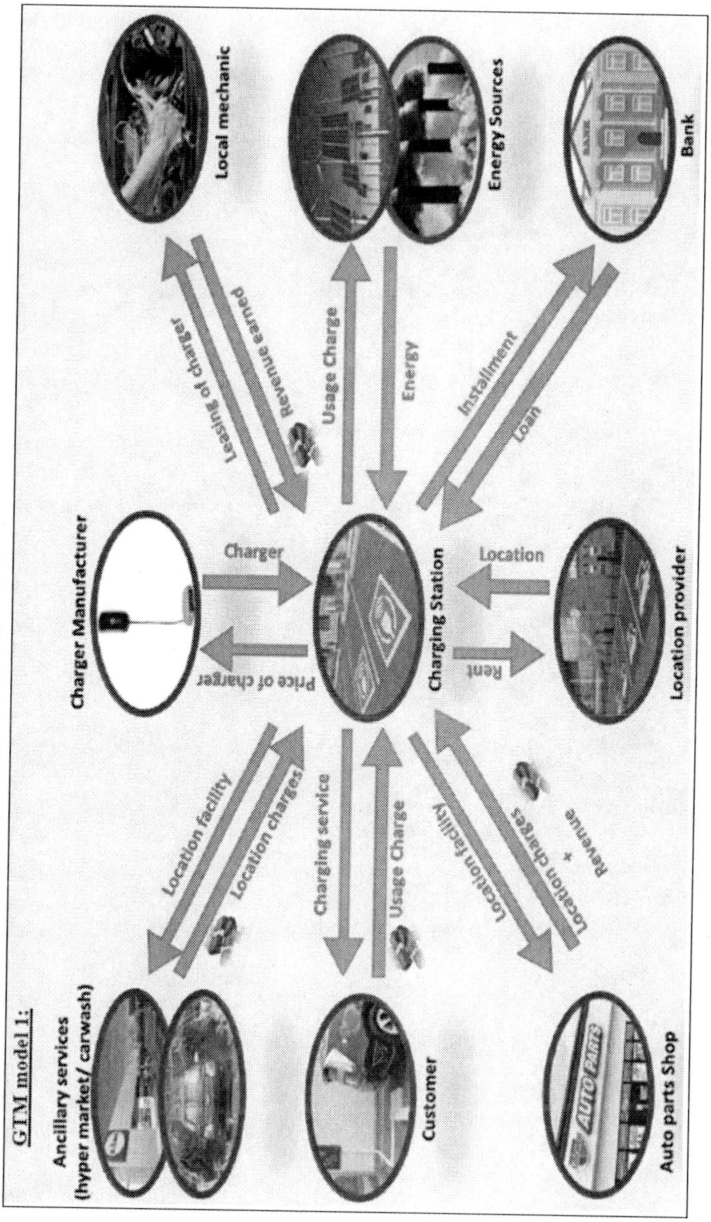

Figure 93: GTM Business Model

Figure 94: Inductive Charging - Business Model

APPENDIX 2

LIST OF EV MANUFACTURERS

S.No.	*Manufacturer*	*Model*	*Top speed*
1		QBeak	90 km/h (56 mph)
2	BMW	i3	150 km/h (93 mph)
3	BMW Brilliance	Zinoro 1E	130 km/h (81 mph)
4	Bolloré	Bluecar	130 km/h (81 mph)
5	BYD	e6	140 km/h (87 mph)
6	Chery	QQ3 EV	
7	Chevrolet	Bolt EV	150 km/h (93 mph) (speed limited)
8	Chevrolet	Spark EV	
9	Citroën	C-Zero	130 km/h (81 mph)
10	COURB	C-ZEN	110 km/h (68 mph)
11	ElectraMeccanica	Solo	132 km/h (82 mph) (limited)
12	Fiat	500e	142 km/h (88 mph)
13	Ford	Focus Electric	135 km/h (84 mph)
14	Girfalco	Azkarra	
15	Honda	Fit EV	148 km/h (92 mph)
16	Hyundai	Ioniq	185 km/h (115 mph)
17	Hyundai	Kona Electric	
18	JAC Motors	JAC J3 EV	120 km/h
19		JAC IEV 6S	130 km/h
20	Kewet	Buddy	80 km/h (50 mph)
21	Kia	Soul EV	145 km/h (90 mph)
22	Kyburz	Kyburz eRodRace	140 km/h
23	Lightning	Lightning GT	200 km/h (124 mph)
24	Mahindra	e2o plus	82 km/h (51 mph)

25	Mahindra	e-Verito	85 km/h (52 mph)
26	Mercedes-Benz	B-Class Electric Drive	160 km/h (99 mph)
27	Microlino	Microlino	90 km/h (56 mph)
28	Mitsubishi	i-MiEV	130 km/h (81 mph)
29	Motores Limpios	Zacua	85 km/h
30	MW Motors	Luka EV	148 km/h (92 mph)
31	Nissan	Leaf	150 km/h (93 mph)
32	Peugeot	i0n	130 km/h (81 mph)
33	Rayttle	E28	80 km/h (50 mph)
34	Renault	Fluence ZE	135 km/h(84 mph), electronically limited
35	Renault	Zoe	135 km/h (84 mph), electronically limited
36	Renault	Twizy	80 km/h (50 mph) (Urban 80 version)
37	Smart	Smart electric drive	125 km/h (78 mph)
38	Sono Motors	Sion	140 km/h (87 mph)
39	Stevens	Zecar	90 km/h (56 mph)
40	Tesla	Model S	209 km/h (130 mph) - 249 km/h (155 mph) (P100D)
41	Tesla	Model X	249 km/h (155 mph) (P100D) - 210 km/h (130 mph)
42	Tesla	Model 3	210 km/h (130 mph) (standard battery) - 225 km/h (140 mph) (long-range battery model)
43	Venturi	Fétish	200 km/h (124 mph)
44	Volkswagen	e-Golf	145 km/h (90 mph)
45	Volkswagen	e-Up!	130 km/h (81 mph)

APPENDIX 3

LIST OF EV CHARGER MANUFACTURERS

S. No.	*EV Charger Manufacturer*
1	AddEnergie Technologies
2	Audi AG
3	Bosch
4	BTC Power
5	ClipperCreek
6	Delphi Automotive Systems
7	Delta Electronics, Inc
8	Dr. Ing. h. c. F. Porsche
9	Eaton Corporation
10	Efacec
11	Eluminocity
12	Evatran
13	EverCharge (Greenit Inc.)
14	EVoCHARGE
15	EVSE LLC (Control Module Ind.)
16	Fuji
17	GridBot, LLC
18	IER
19	JFE Engineering Corporation
20	Juice Bar LLC
21	KebaAG

22	Kyungshin Corporation
23	Kyungshin Corporation
24	Lear Corp.
25	Legrand/Pass & Seymour
26	Leviton
27	Lite-On Clean Energy Technology, Corp
28	meritCharge (eVergo)
29	Milbank
30	Nissan/Sumitomo
31	North Shore Safety
32	Panasonic Corporation (Panasonic Electric Works Co. Ltd.)
33	PEP Stations, LLC
34	Poulsen Hybrid, LLC.
35	Schneider Electric
36	Shanghai Viasystems EMS CO LTD
37	Siemens Energy Inc.
38	Signet Systems, Inc
39	Telefonix, Inc
40	Tesla Motors
41	Tritium PTY LTD
42	Tyco Electronics Corp
43	Wattzilla
44	Yazaki North America, Inc.

APPENDIX 4

LIST OF EV BATTERY MANUFACTURERS

S. No.	Battery Manufactures	Carmaker	Year Founded	Production Capacity	Used in Vehicle	Production Type of Battery
1	A123Systems	Killacycle motorcycle, General Motors (Chevrolet Spark EV), Fisker Automotive (Karma PHEV), Daimler Buses North America (Orion VII), Smith Electric Vehicles electric trucks, Chery Auto, Kandi, Navistar electric trucks, ALTe Powertrain Technologies extended-range EV powertrains, VIA Motorsextended-range VTRUX, three cars with Shanghai Automotive Industry Corp's Roewe brand (an EV, a PHEV and an HEV), BMW (ActiveHybrid 3 and ActiveHybrid 5 hybrid electric vehicles), Mercedes-Benz High Performance Engines (Formula Oneracing Kinetic Energy Recovery System (KERS), Buckeye Bullet land-speed racer	2001	1.5 GWh by 2018	Yes	lithium ion (*lithium iron phosphate*)
2	AESC	Nissan vehicles				Li-ion

S. No.	Battery Manufactures	Carmaker	Year Founded	Production Capacity	Used in Vehicle	Production Type of Battery
3	Altairnano	Phoenix Motorcars, Lightning Car Company, Proterra				Lithium-ion
4	Axeon	Rolls-Royce Motor Cars, Modec, Allied Vehicles, RUF Automobile, Jaguar Cars, Land Rover, Electric Car Corporation				lithium titanate
5	Axion Power International	ePower Engine Systems				lithium iron phosphate
6	Bosch/Samsung	Fiat 500e				lead carbon
7	BYD					
8	Boston Power	Beijing Automotive Group, Saab Automobile				lithium-ion
9	Canbat Batteries	Manufactures automotive batteries including JIS, DIN and BCI				lithium-ion
10	Coslight India	Electric Bus LFP batteries, EV LFP Batteries, E car LFP & NMC batteries				lithium-ion
11	E-One Moli Energy	BMW Mini-E				lithium-ion
12	Electeca	Electric Rickshaw and Electric Van				lithium-ion
13	Electrovaya	Scheduled to provide batteries for future Tatamotors vehicles and Chrysler plug-ins.				lithium-ion

S. No.	Battery Manufactures	Carmaker	Year Founded	Production Capacity	Used in Vehicle	Production Type of Battery
14	EnerDel	Preproduction and prototype batteries for Think Global				lithium-ion
15	Enertech International	Electric Vehicle and Electric Buses batteries				ithium-ion lithium polymer batteries (LiPo)
16	GS Yuasa	Joint ventures with Mitsubishi Motors, and Mitsubishi Corp.; provides batteries for Mitsubishi				lithium-ion
17	Guoxuan High-Tech (Gotion Inc.)	BAIC, SAIC, JAC Motors, Zoyte, Kinglong				Lithium iron phosphate, NMC
18	Johnson Controls	Batteries for Daimler AG, Ford; scheduled to provide batteries for XL Hybrid				lithium-ion battery (Li-ion)
19	K2 Energy Solutions					lithium iron phosphate (LFP)
20	LG Chem	General Motors: Chevrolet VoltGen 1, Gen 2, Chevy Spark, Chevy Bolt, Cadillac ELR Groupe Renault: Renault ZOE, Renault Twizy Hyundai: Hyundai Sonata Hybrid FoMoCo: Ford Focus Electric Volvo Cars:[36][37]Volvo S60 II, Volvo V60,[38]Volvo XC90 II,[39] Volvo S90/V90 II[40]			Yes	lithium-ion

S. No.	Battery Manufactures	Carmaker	Year Founded	Production Capacity	Used in Vehicle	Production Type of Battery
21	Li-Tec Battery GmbH	Batteries for Daimler AG and others				lithium-ion
22	Lian Innovative	Prototype Batteries for IRanKhodro.				lithium-ion
23	Lithium Battery Wale	For All type Of e-Vehicles and e-Rickshaws				lithium-ion
24	Mitsubishi/ GS Yuasa					
25	NEC	Produced prototype batteries for Nissan; Automotive Energy Supply (AESC) is Nissan's joint venture with NEC				lithium-ion
26	Panasonic	Manufactures automotive batteries and cells, mostly for Tesla Motors				
27	Primearth EV Energy Co, a joint venture between Toyota and Matsushita Electric Industrial Co	Future Toyotaproducts				
28	Rexnamo Electro	Batteries for Rexnamo EV's, ULTra Fairwood.	2013			
29	Samsung SDI	Manufactures batteries for BMW and Volkswagen electric carsand plug-in hybrids.				

S. No.	Battery Manufactures	Carmaker	Year Founded	Production Capacity	Used in Vehicle	Production Type of Battery
30	Sanyo	Provides NiMH batteries for Honda and Ford hybrid vehicles and Suzuki Swift				NiMH
31	SB LiMotive					lithium-ion
32	SK Innovation	Kia Soul EV, Daimler A.G. (SLS AMG E-cell), Hyundai (BlueOn)		200MW by 2016	Yes	Lithium polymer battery (LiPo)
33	Tesla	Building gigafactory in joint venture with Panasonic; The Gigafactory 1 planned annual battery production capacity of 35 gigawatt-hours, by 2018				Lithium polymer battery (LiPo)
34	Tianneng					
35	Thunder Sky	For the Tazzari Zero				
36	Valence Technology					lithium ion (lithium iron phosphate)
37	Wanxiang					
38	XALT Energy	Electric buses and marine batteries				lithium ion (lithium iron phosphate)

APPENDIX 5

LIST OF EV MOTORS MANUFACTURERS

Sl. No.	*Name of the motor Manufacturer*
1	Siemens
2	Toshiba
3	ABB
4	Nidec
5	Rockwell Automation
6	Ametek
7	Regal Beloit
8	Johnson Electric
9	Franklin Electric
10	Allied Motion Technologies
11	Faulhaber Group
12	General Electric
13	Danaher Motion
14	WEG
15	Maxon Motor
16	TECO Westinghouse
17	Hitachi
18	Lincolln Electric
19	Piela Electric, Inc
20	Dumore Corporation
21	Kirloskar
22	AVEOX
23	Lynch
24	Netgain Motors, Inc
25	UQM

GLOSSARY OF TERMS

AC Alternating Current- a charge of electricity that regularly changes direction, which is the kind of power that comes from the power plant to homes and businesses.

AER All-Electric Range – the range any EV is able to reach solely using electricity.

Battery Electrochemical cells electrically connected in a series and/or parallel arrangement.

Battery Pack A group of battery cells or modules connected in serial or parallel arrangement, fully configured as a unit meeting the voltage and packaging requirements of a vehicle.

Battery Management System An electronic system within the Vehicle that manages and protects the battery.

Battery System A completely functional complex battery which includes the battery pack and battery support equipment, such as thermal management and battery controls.

BEV Battery Electric vehicle - also known as an "All-electric" vehicle BEV's utilize energy that is stored in rechargeable battery packs. BEV's sustain their power through the batteries and therefore must be plugged into an external electricity source in order to recharge.

BHP "Brake Horsepower" – the actual power output of an engine or motor before any natural losses in power through components such as a gearbox and other ancillaries.

Capacity The total number of ampere hours (Ah) that can be withdrawn from a fully charged cell or battery for a specific set of operating conditions, including discharge rate, temperature, age, stand time, and discharge termination criteria.

Charge (*verb*) Conversion of electrical energy into chemical potential energy within a cell by the passage of a direct current. (*noun*) Coulombs or ampere-hours of energy available in a cell or battery.

Charge Coupling A take-apart transformer for inductive charging operating between 80 kHz and 300 kHz, composed of two primary components—the vehicle inlet and the coupler.

Charger An electrical device that converts alternating current energy to a regulated direct current voltage for replenishing the energy of an energy storage device (i.e., battery) and operating other vehicle electrical systems.

Charging Point A location where electric vehicles can plugged in and charged. These can be at home, at work or in publicly accessible locations.

CCID Charge Circuit Interrupting Device - a safety protection component within an EVSE that reduces the chance of a person getting an electric shock.

Combined Charging System (CCS) Another method to quickly charge electric vehicles through a special electric connection. CCSs often use the SAE J1772, which is the North American electrical standard for Electric Vehicles.

Conductive Coupling A recharge cord and plug that physically connect to the vehicle circuit (see *inductive coupling*).

Connector. A conductive or inductive device that, by insertion into an inlet on the electric vehicle, establishes connection to an electric vehicle for the purpose of energy transfer and information exchange. It is part of a *coupling* (a mating vehicle inlet and connector set).

Controller. A solid-state device that regulates the amount of power delivered to an EV's traction motor.

Coupler. The device connected to the electric vehicle supply equipment that transfers power to the electric vehicle for charging the energy storage system and permits the exchange of information between the EV and the EV's supply equipment. The coupler contains the primary coil of the take-apart transformer, an antenna for communications, a magnet for connection check, and provisions for locking the coupler in the vehicle to prevent tampering.

Coupling. A mating vehicle inlet and connector set.

DC (Direct Current) A charge of electricity that flows in one direction and is the type of power that comes from a battery.

Electric Vehicle (EV). An automotive-type vehicle for highway use, such as passenger automobiles, buses, trucks, vans, and the like, primarily powered by an electric motor that draws current from a rechargeable storage battery, fuel cell, photovoltaic array, or other source of electric current.

Electric Vehicle Supply Equipment (EVSE) The conductors, including the ungrounded, grounded, and equipment grounding conductors, the electric vehicle connectors, attachment plugs, and all other fittings, devices, power outlets, or apparatus installed specifically for the purpose of delivering energy from the premises wiring to the electric vehicle.

EV connector. Off-board component used to interface with the vehicle-mounted EV inlet to supply power and provide communication interface. (The power interface may be conductive, inductive, or other.)

EV cord. The off-board cable containing the conductors to connect the EV plug with the EV power controller to provide power for the vehicle and communications during charge.

EV (Electric Vehicle): A broad category that includes all vehicles that are fully powered by Electricity or an Electric Motor.

EREV (Extended-range electric vehicles) Vehicles that have the ability to run on a gasoline engine if the battery gets low.

EVB (Electric Vehicle Battery): A battery that is used to power the movement of a BEV.

EVD Electric Vehicle Driver.

EV inlet. Vehicle-mounted component which interfaces with the EV connector to receive power and provide communication interface.

Fast Charge Charging at a higher current than a domestic supply (about 7kW as opposed to 3kW). This will fully charge an average electric car in three to four hours. Rapid charging is quicker still.

Ground Fault. Short circuit to ground.

GHG Green House Gas, a gas such as Carbon Dioxide that contributes to global warming through the absorption of infrared radiation.

HCU "Home Charging Unit" - a dedicated charging point for use at home. These incorporate a number of safety features to prevent fires or short circuits and often employ intelligent features such as timers and fast charging. HCU's aren't absolutely necessary but we recommend them for peace of mind.

HEV (Hybrid Electric Vehicles). An HEV utilizes a dual system of electric propulsion and an internal combustion engine.

Hybrid. A car that integrates a small battery and an electric motor to enhance the efficiency of the engine. The battery's charge is maintained by the ICE engine - it cannot be charged by plugging into an electrical supply. Hybrids can offer greater fuel economy than a traditional ICE but can only travel very short distances on electric power only.

ICE (Internal Combustion Engine). An ICE is powered by combustible fuel, often petroleum or natural gas products.

ICEV (Internal Combustion Engine Vehicle). All vehicles that are powered by Fossil Fuels are ICEVs.

IEC 62196. It is a type of connectors that is used to charge Electric Vehicles in Europe.

Inductive Charging System. A charging system that converts low frequency utility power to high frequency, transfers power across a take-apart transformer, and rectifies that power into DC voltage to the batteries.

Inductive Coupling. A recharge cord and plug that uses magnetic induction of electricity to transfer energy to the vehicle rather than using a physical connection (see *conductive coupling*).

Infrastructure. All equipment and facilities required to generate, transmit, distribute, and deliver electricity to an EV.

JEVS G105-1993. Also known as CHAdeMO, it is a method developed to quickly charge Electric Vehicles through the use of a special adapter that delivers up to 62.5 kW. This is used in Japan.

kW (Kilowatt). A unit of electric power.

Level 1 Charging. Charging from a common electrical outlet, which is 120 volts in the United States. The maximum power supplied for Level 1 Charging shall conform to the values shown: Nominal Supply Voltage 120 V. AC single phase; Maximum Continuous Current 12 amps; Branch Circuit Protection 15 amps (minimum); Nominal Continuous Power 1.44 kVA.

Level 2 Charging. High-power charging, which is 240 volts, 40 amps in the United States. The maximum power supplied for Level 2 Charging shall conform to the values shown: Nominal Supply Voltage 208-240 V. AC single phase; Maximum Continuous Current 32 amps; Branch Circuit Protection 40 amps; Nominal Continuous Power 6.66-7.68 kVA.

Level 3 Charging. Fast charging at 480 volts, 400 amps with three-phase power. This energy transfer method utilizes dedicated electric vehicle supply equipment capable of replenishing more than half of the capacity of an EV battery as quickly as in ten minutes. With this method, the electric vehicle accepts dc energy from an off-board power supply. The maximum power supplied for Level 3 charging equipment conforms to these values: Nominal Supply Voltage 600 V dc (maximum); Maximum Continuous Current 400 amps; Branch Circuit Protection As Required; Nominal Continuous Power 160 kW dc.

LIB / Li-ion. Lithium-ion battery, it is a common rechargeable battery. These are the current standard in electric vehicle batteries, offering good energy density, power and fast charging ability. The life of a lithium Ion battery is estimated to be the same as the life of the car (eight to ten years). Of course 'end of life' here does not mean the cars or batteries won't work - after 10 years a lithium ion battery is expected to be at 80% efficiency, so they will still be usable - replacement will be a choice, not a requirement. Should you wish to replace your car's battery, it's possible they will still be in demand as storage devices for renewable energy in industry. They are expensive at the moment, but prices will reduce over time as more EVs hit the road.

Lead Acid Battery. A type of battery used in less modern electric cars. The energy density is much lower than that of lithium Ion batteries, which is the current standard. That means less power output and the need for more frequent charging. Lead acid batteries also have a shorter service life. They are, however, a lot cheaper than lithium ion batteries.

Molten salt battery. A type of battery that utilizes molten salts as an electrolyte.

NEV (Neighborhood Electric Vehicle). BEV's that are limited to streets with lower speed limits, typically around 45mph. NEV's are all-electric and can be recharged using a standard outlet.

NiMH. Nickel Metal Hydride, a less reliable rechargeable battery.

Off Peak Charging. Charging your electrical vehicle at certain lowest cost off-peak hours.

Off-board charger. A charger with the intelligence and control in the charger stand, not on the vehicle.

On-board charger. A charger with the intelligence and control on the vehicle, not in the charger stand.

Photovoltaic Cells (PV). Used on solar panels to convert radiation from the sun into electricity. Solar panels are becoming much more commonplace and can be installed at home to help charge electric cars, allowing true zero-emission motoring and a large cost saving over time.

PHEV (Plug-in Hybrid Electric Vehicles). PHEVs contain a battery that is able to be charged with an external electric power source, PHEV's are a mixture of all electric vehicles and ICEV's.

Pure Electric. A vehicle powered solely by electric motors using power provided by on-board batteries. The batteries are charged using electricity from the national grid.

Range. The maximum distance that an electric vehicle can travel on a single battery charge over a specified driving cycle to the battery manufacturer's recommended maximum discharge level. Alternatively, the distance reached when a specified minimum level of performance or other characteristic (such as battery depth of discharge) is attained.

Rapid Charge. Rapid charging occurs only at dedicated locations and employs a 20-50kW current, allowing an 80% charge of a typical electric car in around 20-30 minutes. Some rapid chargers can top up the remaining 20% at a reduced rate in order to preserve the life of the battery. Regular rapid charging is not good for the long-term life of the battery, but does offer the chance to top up on the occasional longer journey.

Range Anxiety. Worry or stress that is caused due to the fear that an electric car will run out of battery power before the destination is reached.

Regenerative braking. A method of breaking used by EV in which energy from the braking of the vehicle is stored and used.

RPM. "Revolutions Per Minute" - the number of times the shaft of an electric motor turns through 360 degrees in one minute.

SAE J1772. The standard North American electrical connection for Electric Vehicles. Generally works with Level 1 and Level 2 systems.

Time-of-use (TOU) rates. Discounted electricity rates established by utilities to encourage use of electricity during off-peak hours.

Tesla Supercharger. A super-fast charging system that can provide up to 120 kW directly to the car's battery. Currently these systems are only available to Teslas.

Three-phase electric power. In an AC motor in an electric vehicle, three-phase current is used instead of single phase, as it generates a rotating magnetic field from zero RPM and is typically 150% more efficient in the same power range. In other words, high torque at zero revs is made possible by a three-phase system on an AC motor.

Vehicle Inlet. The device on the electric vehicle into which the connector is inserted for energy transfer and information exchange. This is part of the charge coupling.

V2G. Vehicle-to-Grid, a system that allows Electric Vehicles to communicate with the power grid to manage the flow of electricity in either direction.

VRLA battery. Valve-regulated lead-acid battery, a rechargeable lead-acid battery.

W2W. "Well-to-Wheel" - measuring the CO_2 emissions of a car, taking into account the production of the fuel or electricity. This is a fair analysis of the impact on the environment of electric vehicles, as they have zero emissions at point of use but clearly have an environmental impact earlier in the chain. However, for a fair comparison with an ICE vehicle, W2W must also be calculated in the drilling of the oil, refining and transportation, not just the tailpipe emissions. Taking this into account, an average electric vehicle will produce 80g/km of CO_2 compared with 147-161g/km for an ICE.

INDEX